SEVEN TIMES DOWN, EIGHT TIMES UP:
LANDING ON YOUR FEET IN AN UPSIDE DOWN WORLD

Dr. Alan Gettis, Ph.D.

Trafford Publishing

May you always
land on your feet.

Alan Gettis, PhD

Printed in Victoria, Canada

National Library of Canada Cataloguing in Publication

Gettis, Alan, 1944-
        Seven times down, eight times up : landing on your feet in an upside down world / Alan Gettis.
Includes bibliographical references.
ISBN 1-4120-0514-0
        I. Title.

BF632.G47 2003   158.1   C2003-903567-0

TRAFFORD

This book was published *on-demand* in cooperation with Trafford Publishing.
On-demand publishing is a unique process and service of making a book available for retail sale to the public taking advantage of on-demand manufacturing and Internet marketing.
On-demand publishing includes promotions, retail sales, manufacturing, order fulfilment, accounting and collecting royalties on behalf of the author.

Suite 6E, 2333 Government St., Victoria, B.C. V8T 4P4, CANADA
Phone   250-383-6864   Toll-free   1-888-232-4444 (Canada & US)
Fax   250-383-6804   E-mail   sales@trafford.com
Web site   www.trafford.com   TRAFFORD PUBLISHING IS A DIVISION OF TRAFFORD HOLDINGS LTD.
Trafford Catalogue #03-0883   www.trafford.com/robots/03-0883.html

10   9   8   7   6   5   4   3   2

I dedicate this book
to my wife, Nan
who is perfect
just the way she is.

Contents

Acknowledgements

I learned early on about the power that stories have to stir, teach, move, and truly engage the listener. My father, George, was a wonderful story teller. As a boy and young man, I was fascinated by those stories regardless of whether they were fictional, real, or embellished.

Since 1969, I have worked with thousands of patients and am thankful to them for the many lessons they have taught me. Many times when I deemed myself to be brilliant with the psychological jargon I was spouting, I noticed my patients were looking sleepy or bored. But whenever I told them stories, they perked up and could immediately relate to them.

I have been blessed with very loving and supportive people in my life, and I have immense gratitude. They certainly have contributed to the essence of this book. My mother, Betty, instilled in me the idea of reaching for the stars and the feeling that I could definitely reach them.

I am grateful to my wife, Nan. After thirty four years of marriage, I am still nurtured by her never ending encouragement and love.

My children, Jenna and David, have helped me grow in countless ways and I am as thankful as I can possibly be for them. David did most of the typing and editing of the various drafts of this book and also produced the cover design.

I'd also like to thank my brothers, Sam, Rip, and Bruce, and my sister Harriet, for their enthusiasm and ideas. And, to

the esteemed authors, Dr. Joseph Luciani and Dr. Sam Menahem, thank you for the many ways you've contributed to this
book.

Introduction

There is a proverb in Japan that states "Nanakorobi Yao-ki".

> Nana = Seven
> Korobi = Fall Down
> Ya = Eight
> Oki = Stand Up

The proverb translates to, "Seven times down, eight times up". It derives its origins from okiagari dolls, paper-mache toys that when knocked down, always return to an upright position. The dolls have no arms or legs and are also known as Daruma dolls.

Daruma (also known as Bodhidharma) was the first patriarch of Zen. He traveled from India to China in the sixth century. Legend has it that he sat in a cave meditating for nine years without moving, in order to obtain enlightenment. In the process, his legs withered to nothing and his hands shriveled away from lack of use. But he remained steadfast and seemed to get healthier with the passing years. Folklore suggests he finally died after vitally living eight hundred thirteen years.

The armless, legless Daruma dolls are weighted so they always pop up after being pushed down. They represent the resiliency and perseverance of Daruma. They stand for success after misfortune. Daruma dolls inspire you to rise no matter how many times you stumble or fall down. "Nana" in Japanese has a double meaning. It means "seven" but is also used to denote "many".

So, "Nanakorobi Yaoki", or "Seven times down, eight times up", is a call to never give up. It is a celebration of your spirit, determination, and ability to not only land on your feet, but to also evolve, enjoy, thrive, and transcend.

SEVEN TIMES DOWN, EIGHT TIMES UP:
LANDING ON YOUR FEET IN AN UPSIDE DOWN WORLD

The Stories

Even Monkeys Fall Out of Trees

A Japanese proverb has it that "even monkeys fall out of trees." Just yesterday, I locked myself out of my car. Although I'd categorize myself as fairly intelligent, it seems that every contestant on Jeopardy knows more answers than I do. When I lectured to college students and deemed myself rather fascinating, I couldn't help but notice that some students were falling asleep. Despite being a decent athlete, I'm almost always one of the most rigid, awkward skiers on the slopes. And I forgot to mention that my nose is rather large.

When I have "one of those days" or incidents when it becomes obvious to me (and maybe to others) that I'm not the coolest, suavest, smartest, or nicest human being on the planet, I still try to remember that I'm O.K. I give myself the benefit of the doubt, and if there's anything to be learned from the experience, I'll try to digest the lesson. One definition of intelligence is that it is the ability to profit from experience.

There's nothing wrong with wanting to improve yourself. In fact, striving to become more like the person you would like to be is healthy and validates the notion that you are not a static entity and that you are capable of making changes. Just don't judge yourself too harshly while you're trying to bring about those changes. The best figure skaters in the world still fall on their behinds. Rocket scientists' formulas are sometimes way off the mark. Most of us don't resemble models, and de-

5

spite what Andy Warhol stated, most of us don't even get our fifteen minutes of fame.

The best major league baseball players who make many millions of dollars each year have batting averages of about .300. This means that they do not get hits 7 of every 10 times they come up to bat. Another way of looking at this is that they fail to achieve their goal 70% of the time. And these are the best players in the world. Yes, even monkeys fall out of trees.

Letting Go

Psychologists use the term "perseveration" to describe a person's inability to shift from one task to another. A person who is unable to leave a particular mental set behind so as to get on with something new or different is said to be perseverating. It is possible to perseverate emotionally. People hold on to negative feelings and self-defeating thoughts. They cling to these in such a way that they taint day-to-day interactions and happenings. The opposite of this "holding on" is "letting go".

It's rumored that in India, monkeys are caught in a very unusual way. A narrow neck basin filled with nuts is put in the ground. The monkey puts his hands in the narrow neck basin and fills them with nuts. The monkey can't remove his thick fists and keeps holding the nuts while the trappers close in. The monkey, focused on the nuts, holds on tightly while the trappers move in and catch him. The monkey didn't know when it was time to let go.

We human beings also have trouble knowing when it is time to let go. Our tendency is to cling to thoughts that are non-productive and/or self-defeating. We all beat the proverbial dead horse. And then, we beat him again, and again. What thoughts are you clinging to that you could work toward letting go of? What thoughts are you clinging to that are creating anger, anxiety, or depression? Take a mental inventory.

Many years ago, I learned to drive a car with a manual transmission. It wasn't easy learning how to shift gears. I stalled, got stuck on occasions, and felt like giving up. It was a lot easier to drive an automatic. But with repeated efforts, I learned the skills necessary to shift gears and move on, albeit not always as smoothly as I would have liked. Don't automatically do what you always do. You may need to learn to shift gears, so you don't get stuck (emotionally speaking) and so you can move on. It requires practice and patience. It also requires the recognition that holding on holds you back and interferes with your ability to enjoy each day as much as you possibly can.

A well-known Zen story tells of two monks walking in a heavy rain on a dirt road. They came upon a young woman in a silk kimono who was unable to cross a very muddy section. The one monk swiftly lifted her and carried her over the mud. The two monks continued on their way, walking in silence until hours later when they approached the monastery grounds.

The second monk could no longer restrain himself, and said, "What's wrong with you? We monks don't go near women, especially not young and lovely ones. Why did you do that?"

To which the first monk replied, "I put her down hours ago. Are you still carrying her?"

Out With the Old, In With the New

Somewhere in your head there is a small perch. On that perch resides what I refer to as your "critical tenant". That tenant began to be formed in early childhood. It may be one person, such as your father, or mother, or grandparent. More likely, it is a composite of various key people in your life who you have felt criticized, rejected, or abandoned by. People who have deceived you, diminished you, or were disappointed in you. These people may or may not be alive today. It doesn't matter in the sense that he, she, or they are still in your head, on that perch, ready to pick you apart at any moment. Like a vulture readying itself to attack, your critical tenant hovers waiting for the right time to ravage you.

Fears and insecurities left over from childhood continue to color our feelings even though they took place a long time ago. Those negative themes are played over and over again in our heads. Picture them playing on scratchy, old 45 and 78 RPM records, or on old worn out cassette tapes. It is time to throw them out and substitute new compact discs (CD's) that are efficient, effective, enthusiastic, and encouraging. CD's with messages of acceptance, worthiness, patience, and tolerance. Optimism, hopefulness, forgiveness, and love.

Whoever makes up your "critical tenant" has spent enough time inside your head. The jig is up. It's time for you to clean house. It's time for you to evict that tenant and firmly put up a sign on that perch in your head that says:

"For use and enjoyment of owner only. Not for sale or rent!"

The Prison of Conditioning

As a psychologist, I strongly believe that people are capable of making significant changes. When people offer statements such as "That's the way I am", or "I wish I could be different, but I can't", or "I was born that way", or "It's my nature to be like this", I talk to them about the phenomenon of conditioning.

There is a story about a hunter who captured a small bear cub and put it in a cage that was six feet long. The hunter decided not to feed the cub unless it walked the length of the cage, turned around, and walked back – six feet forward and six feet backward. The cub was hungry and restless. He walked up and back the length of his cage and promptly got fed by the hunter. This satisfied the cub and pleased the hunter. This behavior took place 3 times a day for many years.

One day, a tornado hurled the cage into the woods and the door blew off. The bear walked out of the cage and was alone in the woods. The hunter was not there. After slowly assessing the situation, the bear walked six feet forward and six feet backward, six feet forward and six feet backward, six feet forward and six feet backward...

Even though we are adults, we still let the conditioning of our past dominate us. We don't recognize our freedom, but now actually self-impose the ideas and regulations that made us feel so badly. Yes, we walk six feet forward and six feet backward. We have been taught our entire lives to think, feel, and behave in certain ways. Many of these teachings hold us back or interfere with the quality of our lives. It is possible to be different, even to break life-long patterns. Stop believing you cannot change. When you say or think, "I can't", you are denying your freedom to choose and respond differently. Stop functioning on automatic pilot.

The noted psychologist Rollo May has defined freedom as "the pause between stimulus and response". In that gap, you can dare to be different, decide upon a new way of thinking, or pursue a course of action that would typically run counter to your usual way of responding. Instead of stimulus – response again and again, it's now stimulus – pause and make an active conscious decision as an evolving, choosing human being – response. You can free yourself from your conditioning and make choices that no longer contribute to keeping you from feeling as good as you can. You can stop walking six feet forward and six feet backward.

<u>The Meaning of Life</u>

Sometimes I think we make life a bit more complicated than it need be. My bias is to try to keep things fairly simple and recognize when I'm unnecessarily complicating things. I no longer try to figure out the major questions of life such as:

Why are we here?

What is the meaning of life?

What happens when we die?

Instead of doing that, I try to accept that the universe is paradoxical, unpredictable, and enigmatic, and that "that is that". Of course, as usual, this is easier said than done.

Let me tell you a story about my friends Sam and Susan. Sam has always been interested in the mystical, the supernatural, the paranormal, and the transcendental. He has keenly pursued reincarnation and past life regression. He has spent many hours (or is it lifetimes?) wondering about the metaphysical. Susan doesn't share Sam's interest in these other-world matters. She's got her feet firmly planted on this earth and is more concerned with meeting her daily responsibilities involving many things including work and motherhood.

One spring evening, as Sam sat in the rocking chair in his living room, he repeatedly asked himself the same question. "What is the meaning of life?" Over and over, "What is the meaning of life?". Hoping for some 'Aha' experience, some

13

cosmic sign, some divine intervention, he sat for a long time repeating the question.

All of a sudden, he heard a booming voice! It came from the kitchen. It was Susan, yelling, "Sam, what color should we paint the kitchen?".

It hit Sam like a thunderbolt. His question had been answered. "What is the meaning of life?"

It could have been any reply of Susan's that offered the answer. She could have said, "We're having dinner at 7 o'clock" or "Paul and Anne are coming over".

The point was that the meaning of life was right there, right then. It was staring him in the face the whole time. To participate fully, consciously, and responsibly. To see that everything that happens is part of the answer. The meaning of life is to live fully in this lifetime, here and now.

Browsing through a notebook that I kept in the early 70's, I came across the following poem (author unknown).

This is It
and I am It
and You are It
and So is That
and He is It
and She is It
and It is It
and That is That.

Where Are You Looking?

I like to tell stories. People resonate with them to the degree they are ready and able to. They mean different things to different people. I frequently tell the following story and it seems to impact on everyone a little differently.

One night while walking in the city, I saw a woman on her hands and knees, apparently looking for something under a street lamp. She was receptive to my offer to help her look for an "important key" that she had lost. After crawling around for about fifteen minutes on my hands and knees, I asked her, "Are you sure you lost the key right here?"

She replied, "Oh no, I lost it several blocks from here."

Puzzled, I asked, "Then why are you looking here?"

She answered, "Because the light is much brighter here," and then continued her search.

Sometimes we seek answers or fulfillment in safe, well-lit places so to speak, rather than to venture in the darker, more risky or challenging areas. For example, looking for job fulfillment while staying at a "dead-end", rather unsatisfying job that you've been at for years may be more preferable to you than taking the risk of changing jobs (perhaps to a place several blocks away to get back to the story mentioned above).

I'm reminded of the old story about a peasant who's looking for his missing donkey while he's riding it. (That's the whole story!) Or, have you ever tried to find your glasses when they were sitting on top of your head the whole time? If you are seeking answers, looking for happiness, intimacy, self-worth, or satisfaction, "Where are you looking?" is a very relevant question.

The Winner

A friend of mine recently ran in a popular five-mile race. The race organizers raffled off several prizes afterwards. The grand prize was two round trip airline tickets to anyplace in the United States. They would call out a number and if it matched the one on your running bib (that is worn during the run), you won the prize. You had to be present to win.

They called, "213". This happened to be my friend's house number, but not her bib number. No one claimed the prize. They re-announced it, "213". Nothing doing. They drew another number. It was "496", her number. She screamed in joy, ran on the stage, got the prized envelope, and triumphantly held it above her head. Thoughts of San Francisco danced in her head. Life was good.

After milling around and accepting congratulations for a few minutes, she began making her way through the crowd of runners. All of a sudden, her eyes widened. She was looking at a man who was wearing the running bib numbered 213. She remembered that it was the original number called because it was the same as her house number. A whirlwind of mixed emotions evidenced themselves immediately. Not yielding to the impulse to keep walking, she stopped and said to the man, "This belongs to you. I guess you weren't around when they called your winning number. It's a plane trip wherever you want to go. Have fun. Congratulations."

When I was a young boy, I remember my father matter-of-factly telling me, "Always do the right thing and you'll never go wrong". He said, "You'll know what the right thing is." Fifty years later, I can honestly say his simplistic shared wisdom was right on target.

Here's an interesting footnote. When runner #213 thanked my friend, she noticed that his manner of speaking indicated some type of problem. As she walked away, she glanced back to see the man talking to a woman in sign language. He had never heard 213 being called because he was deaf. In a different kind of way, my friend felt even happier than she did when she thought she was going to San Francisco. Life was still good. Maybe, life was even better. And, in my book, she was most definitely a winner!

Practice What You Preach

Years ago, I attended a staff meeting at a mental health center. One of the therapists was discussing a 60 year-old depressed woman that she was working with. There had been a minimum of improvement despite three months of therapy. A staff psychiatrist advocated electroshock therapy (ECT). In case you are not familiar with ECT, suffice it to say it should be used only as a last resort. Powerful shocks are delivered to the person's brain numerous times. It is a very disturbing sight to see.

After the meeting, I sought the psychiatrist out and privately asked him, "If this was your mother, would you want her to receive electroshock?" He was taken aback by the question. To his credit, he said that he'd think about it and tell me the next day. He did. He told me that if his mother was in a similar situation to the 60 year-old woman described above, he would not want her to get ECT.

I try to only ask others to do what I would be willing to do myself. I only make recommendations that I would be willing to comply with. You know the old line about practicing what you preach. Try to narrow the gap between what you say and what you do. A good rule of thumb is to only ask of others what you would be willing to do yourself.

Legend has it that a woman and her eight year old son once traveled a long distance to get help from Mahatma Gandhi. The woman wanted Gandhi to tell her son to stop eating sugar. The boy's teeth were full of cavities, his behavior was ill mannered, and he generally didn't feel well. Gandhi did not offer any advice but instructed them to return in a month. The disappointed woman and her son did come back a month later. Gandhi looked at the boy and said, "It is best that you stop eating sugar." The woman was grateful but puzzled and asked Gandhi why he couldn't have said that a month ago. He replied, "Madam, a month ago, I was eating sugar."

Use What You Have

Each day is probably at least a bit different from every other day. And some days are better than others. Today, for no apparent reason, I woke with a very stiff neck. I went to bed last night with the intention of getting up early, running a few miles, and working out at a local gym. Waking with a stiff neck I decided that rather than exercise, I would exercise good judgment and write this story instead.

Our circumstances are always changing. Nothing stays the same. We can count on it. Sometimes we are alone. Other times we are with loved ones, or strangers. At times we enjoy good health and at times we struggle with an array of symptoms reflective of illness or imbalance. Our bodies continue to change as do our mental faculties.

Bernard Glassman, a Zen Master, talks about making the best use of the ingredients you have to work with on any particular day. It's like making soup. If you have carrots, potatoes, celery, kidney beans, water, onions, salt, pepper, spinach, and cauliflower, you won't be able to make chicken noodle soup. But you will be able to make a delicious vegetable bean soup. At any given time, you will have a different set of ingredients available. Always use what you have to make the best possible soups you can. Do not feel compelled to use every ingredient at hand. You can decide the soup may be better if you leave one or two ingredients out.

For example, you may be angry one day but may decide not to use that ingredient in your soup. Today, my soup does not include running or exercise at the gym. I'm working with everything I have available today to prepare a soup that's nutritious, tasty, and satisfying.

Each day, take stock of what you have available. You have lots of ingredients to use that you may not even realize. Use what you have and don't focus on what you could have cooked up if only you had other ingredients. What you have is plenty. Your ingredient list may change daily, and may even change numerous times during the day. Experiment with using the ingredients in creative ways. Writing this story is one of the ingredients in the soup I'm making today. Excuse me, I have to stir the pot!

You Are Not Dead

A middle-aged woman came to my office one afternoon and simply stated, "I'm dead." No matter what I asked her, she only replied, "I'm dead."

Finally, out of exasperation and bewilderment, I said, "You sit here and speak just like a live person. Are there any differences between a dead person and a live one? If there aren't, it really doesn't matter whether you are dead or alive!"

She immediately responded, "Dead people don't bleed."

I quickly went to the desk drawer and got a sterile needle. I popped her finger with it and a drop of blood came to the surface. Feeling exceptionally clever, I smugly asked, "What do you think now?"

She looked with astonishment at her finger and answered, "Oh my gosh, dead people *do* bleed!"

This story did not actually happen to me. It is a story told in the field of mental health to illustrate how people sometimes cling to certain beliefs, even in the face of physical, visual, behavioral, or sensual evidence to the contrary.

There are beauty pageant winners who think they are unattractive. There are very intelligent people who do not feel smart. You may cling to a belief that you're too this or not enough that. It's possible that you will misinterpret what transpires so as to support your core beliefs about yourself. There are people who don't believe others are sincere when they are complimented by them because it doesn't fit their belief system. What beliefs are you holding onto that create low self-esteem, guilt, anxiety, or depression? What beliefs are you holding onto despite any and all evidence to the contrary? I've worked with hundreds of people in therapy in which the only things that had to be "cured" were the false beliefs they held about themselves.

Give Yourself A Chance

Courage has been defined as the ability to proceed in spite of anxiety. Life becomes very restrictive when you let anxiety dictate what you do or do not do. When you avoid more and more situations, your world becomes somewhat safer but also much narrower. This avoidance-oriented lifestyle is sometimes referred to as neurosis.

Maslow distinguished between "fear choices" and "growth choices". Decisions where the reduction of anxiety is the primary motivating factor are called fear choices. They are much easier to make than are growth choices, which are decisions in which the primary motivation is to reach potentials and achieve gratification. It is always much easier to make the fear choice. It is much safer and less anxiety provoking to do so. Fear choices lead to "miserable safety". They narrow your world and lead to emotional disturbances or lives of quiet desperation.

Think carefully before you answer. Do the choices you make lead to a life of miserable safety? I know it's less complicated to simply continue with the status quo or the known quantity. Is your fear that if you rock the boat, it will sink and that you don't have a life preserver? Do you feel trapped in a situation or relationship that saddens you? If you continue to make fear choices motivated by anxiety reduction, you will most likely get instant emotional replay.

Growth choices involve risk. Yet, the only way you can get what you want from life is through making growth choices. Each day you'll have plenty of opportunity to decide between fear choices and growth choices. Take a chance. In the Wizard of Oz, the scarecrow said, "I try to stay away from matches but I'd face a whole boxful if I had a chance of getting some brains."

Ghouls, Goblins, and Things that Go Bump in the Night

Darkness has always been associated with evil and frightening things. Think of all the horror movies you've seen. Most of the scenes that make you scream or gasp take place at night. Dracula never showed his face in the daytime. In the musical 'Phantom of the Opera', there is a song about the "phantom of the night". As little children, many of us were scared of the dark. We preferred to go to sleep with the lights on or at the very least to have a night light (trying to light the darkness and feel safer). Even as adults, nightlights can be comforting.

My sister-in-law Diane and I have independently observed that the eeriest hour is from 3:00 a.m. to 4:00 a.m. It is likely that you have woken from a nightmare during this time. Or, perhaps you woke to strange noises in the house. If your phone rings during this hour, I can get you the name of a good cardiologist.

It's easy to imagine all sorts of scary things in the dark. The light is very reassuring, be it the light of day or the artificial light of bulbs. And, remember God said, "Let there be light". That was a most powerful statement and experience. With all of this talk of darkness and light, I am also talking metaphorically. Regardless of the time of day, it can indeed be a dark time for us if we are scared, anxious, or distressed.

Remember when you were a little kid and it was dark and you believed there were ghosts or monsters in your room. You really believed it, and it was only when your mom or dad flicked that light on and you looked all around that you began to feel relief and more secure. And, maybe they kept that light on until you fell back asleep.

Now, when you lose your way, feel frightened and insecure, I want you to picture yourself flicking the light switch on. You are in control of the light switch. Practice picturing yourself doing this and seeing that the ghosts, ghouls, and monsters are not there when you shed light on the situation, just like when you were a small child.

I want you to empower yourself by saying, "Let there be light."

<u>May Be</u>

It is difficult to predict how things might turn out. There are so many spontaneous twists and turns in life, in a year, in a month, sometimes even in an hour. Just when we think we know exactly what's going to happen, something else might spring up. As intuitive as we might be, inevitably some of our expectations don't come to pass. We continually need to cultivate our ability to be flexible and adapt.

It is not uncommon to react impulsively and/or overreact to situations and events that we experience. We may quickly feel disgust, disappointment, frustration, rage, elation, or despair. How often have you said or felt like saying, "Why me?".

There is a Taoist story of a farmer whose horse ran away. That evening his neighbors gathered at his farmhouse to offer their condolences on his bad luck. He said, "May be." The following day, the horse returned and brought with it six wild horses. All the neighbors came by to congratulate the farmer on his good fortune. He said, "May be."

The next morning his sixteen year-old son tried to ride one of the wild horses. He was thrown and broke his leg. Again the neighbors came to offer their sympathy for his misfortune. The farmer said, "May be." The following afternoon, army officers came to the village to seize young men to fight in an unjust war. The farmer's son was rejected because of his broken leg. When the neighbors came in to say how fortunate everything had turned out, the farmer said, "May be."

We can live life passionately and deeply without over-reacting to every new development that seems to offer obstacles to hurdle. Keep this story in mind. When some-thing happens and your first inclination is to say "Why me", see if instead you can possibly say "May be".

A Tale of Two Secretaries

This is the story of two secretaries sitting fifteen feet apart at their desks in a law office. Jennifer and Sarah have worked there for about a year. Ms. Fullerton, one of their bosses walks in and as she passes Jennifer's desk, Jennifer says good morning. They engage in cordial small talk for a minute. Fifteen feet later, Sarah and Ms. Fullerton exchange smiles and early morning greetings.

Later in the morning, Mr. Phillips (another boss) arrives and Jennifer says good morning to him as he goes by her desk. A few seconds later, Sarah offers her good morning. Mr. Phillips says nothing to either of them. Here's where the plot thickens. Jennifer feels miserable the rest of the morning. She's turning things over in her head again and again, fretting, worrying, and wondering what she may have done to disappoint Mr. Phillips.

Did she neglect to do something important or do a poor job on that last report she turned in? Is he leaning toward getting rid of her before her one year review and the raise she was hoping for? She feels insecure, nervous, frightened, and is unable to concentrate.

Sarah, who was equally snubbed, feels fine the rest of the morning. She does not take Mr. Phillips' lack of response personally, but rather believes it to mean that he is simply preoccupied or not in a good morning mood. Humming away at her computer, she's able to focus on the tasks at hand.

31

In essence, Jennifer did not empower herself emotionally speaking. It was as if she said, "Okay Mr. Phillips, how am I going to feel today? It isn't up to me, it's up to you. If you look at me cross eyed or don't give me a cheery good morning, I'll feel rotten and edgy the rest of the day. If you smile or give me a nice greeting, I'll feel fine. So what's it going to be for me today Mr. Phillips? How am I going to feel? It's not up to me, it's up to you!"

Sarah decided herself how she was going to feel. Jennifer left it up to Mr. Phillips and therefore placed herself in an emotionally vulnerable position. Ultimately, Jennifer needs to discover that she can decide to feel good even though Mr. Phillips may not feel good on that particular day. Whether he says good morning or not is really not the issue. The issue is what Jennifer says to herself and how she decides to respond no matter what Mr. Phillips says or does not say.

Because people do not act according to your wishes or preferences doesn't mean life stinks or your world is about to fall apart. The moral of this story is that Mr. Phillips didn't make Jennifer miserable. She made herself miserable. Empower yourself emotionally.

The Last Man Standing

A guy I worked with in therapy told me that he suffered from "the last man standing syndrome". In all my years as a clinician, I have never heard that term put forth as a diagnosis. He explained that if he got into any kind of an argument or even a disagreement, he would do anything he could to win. In effect, he would go to any means to be the last one standing at the end of the fight. He wasn't talking about physical harm, although it had sometimes come down to that. But, usually it was brutal hard-hitting verbal and psychological warfare. He did this mostly with people he loved, in particular with his wife.

The closer the relationship was, the more potential ammunition he had available to him. He knew his wife's history, her weaknesses and vulnerabilities. He knew precisely which buttons to push and how to diminish her as a person. If she'd respond in kind, trying desperately to defend herself by going on the attack, he would bring out the heavy artillery and go for the kill. His philosophy indeed was despite all costs, it would be he who was the last man standing.

If you are angry, you may want to say something that hurts the other person. This is always a large mistake that only creates further problems. Name calling, blaming, and bringing up the past again and again simply create more bad feelings. They certainly do not solve the issues at hand. Expressing your anger spontaneously is not always a good idea

33

because it is hard to be rational when you're consumed with rage.

I'm not advocating that you bury your head in the sand and do not deal with the situations provoking your anger. Rather, I'm suggesting that it would be in your (and the other person's) best interest to pause, count to 100, breathe deeply, and think about the salient points you'd like to get across and how to do so. If some time passes, it's also conceivable that the person you're upset with may be more willing and able to hear and absorb your concerns.

The passage of even a short amount of time can be helpful. Sometimes, it may be best to wait a day or so to deal with a very inflammatory situation. Don't get entrenched in your foxholes. Instead of being the last man standing, try to be the first person pausing, counting, breathing…

A Work In Progress

It was in the late 1960's and I was trying to finish up my doctorate at the New School for Social Research in the Greenwich Village section of New York. The Vietnam War was raging and the government decided to stop honoring student deferments. I was drafted. I never really knew what insomnia was until then. In a blink of an eye, my life had been turned upside down.

One minute I was a graduate student spending a lot of time exploring the galleries and coffee houses of New York, with a promising future and a girlfriend I was considering getting married to. Then, all of a sudden, I was transformed into a sleepless, dispirited, unemployed soldier to be, who would have to leave his family and girlfriend and perhaps go off to war. I was anything but a happy camper. In fact, I was quite discouraged.

On my first day of basic training, I had some trouble with the rigorous physical demands. I was a bit overweight and out of shape. I was already lonely and was feeling quite sorry for myself when our drill sergeant singled me out for some attention. He put his face about one inch from mine and screamed at the top of his lungs, "Gettis, you're a worthless piece of crap!". That was my life in the army – chapter one.

Years later, when I was able to look back somewhat objectively, I was able to appreciate those two years in the military. After my advanced infantry training in Fort Lewis, Washington (I got to spend time around Seattle), I was assigned to duty in an army hospital and got invaluable experience as a psychologist. I made some good friendships, did some traveling, and later married (that same girl) and finished up my schooling using the benefits from the G.I. bill.

So, although chapter one had me near hitting bottom, subsequent chapters slowly but surely built toward a happy ending. I guess that's evidence for a "You never know" philosophy. I think it was Kierkegaard who said that life must be lived forwards but it can only be understood backwards.

You are a work in progress. Despite the content of any previous chapters in your life's book, there are other chapters to be written. You are the primary author of that book. Others may collaborate with you, but it is your book and the final lines will always be written by you. If you are in the midst of a disheartening chapter, keep the bigger picture in mind as you begin to expect and author more fulfilling chapters in the future.

It's Always Here and Now

In *Alice In Wonderland,* the Queen admonishes Alice to obey the rule which is…

> Jam tomorrow,
> and Jam yesterday –
> but never Jam today.

Although it is jam every other day, somehow today is never a jam day. The focus on the past and on the future taints the present. We sometimes dwell on where we've been or where we are going to the extent that the present is diminished. Yet, it is not yesterday and not tomorrow. It is today. It is here and now.

You can always answer the question "Where am I?" with the answer "Here". You can always answer the question "What time is it?" with the answer "Now". The 1960's phrase "Be here now" means being fully where you are at, not simply physically, but also in terms of your consciousness. If you are dwelling too much in the past or future you will not be fully conscious in the present.

There is a story about 2 guys who can't agree how to spend their Friday night. They decide to go their separate ways. One goes to the synagogue. The other goes to a party. The guy who went to the party is there, but he's not there fully. He's thinking about his friend at the synagogue and how this friend had made a good decision. The guy at the synagogue is thinking about the party he's missing and all the fun his friend must be having. Either guy could have had an enjoyable experience, but neither did.

Invest yourself and your consciousness fully in being where you are. Don't do things half-heartedly, but rather whole heartedly. Once you decide to do something, do it as best as you can without second guessing. Rewrite the rule. Jam today!

Forgiveness

Is there someone who hurt you deeply? Betrayed you? Abused you? Is there someone who took advantage of you? Abandoned you? Did someone malign you? Mistreat you? Do you still harbor anger, rage, or resentment? If so, it could be damaging to your emotional well-being and your physical health. Holding on to those powerful feelings for a long time can compromise you on many different levels. This is the stuff ulcers, headaches, high blood pressure, unhappiness, and despair use for building blocks.

It was most likely someone close to you who wronged you. Perhaps a relative, parent, a lover, or a friend. As you know, holding on to negative emotions is not a principle of good mental health. Letting go is. If possible, I would like you to consider forgiving the person who hurt you. This is an action that will empower you. It is a humane and generous action in the spirit of giving.

Forgive is a word made up of 2 words, for and give. Together they equate to a proactive process of granting, remitting, pardoning, and yielding. Forgiving is a very active process of letting go of stockpiled negativity and getting on with your life so that your day to day experiences are neither distorted nor spoiled by your past resentments. If you forgive someone, you will be freeing a lot of energy that can be utilized in the interest of having a more productive and enjoyable life.

39

Aside from forgiving someone for his or her past transgressions against you, there's another act of forgiveness that is equally important. To forgive yourself is a compassionate and healing action. Think carefully about your own behaviors, attitudes, and relationships over the course of your lifetime. If there is anything you feel very troubled about, in your mind, ask for forgiveness, and forgive yourself.

There were twin sisters who became involved with the same young man in college. It became a highly charged, competitive situation that lead to the sisters not talking to each other for several years. They had a mutual friend who realized the pain of both sisters. This friend went to each sister with the tale that the other sister had a terminal illness. She arranged a meeting of the twins. When they laid eyes on each other, they ran into each other's arms and simultaneously said, "I'm sorry". They truly meant it. They forgave each other. They forgave the friend. And, they forgave themselves.

<u>Dealing With Anxiety</u>

If you struggle with anxiety attacks, it may be at least some small solace to know you have a lot of company. Millions of others also grapple with severe anxiety or panic attacks. It is an understatement to say these attacks are usually frightening. People typically believe they are dying or going crazy. They fear losing control and winding up in mental institutions. Keep the following in mind. Your worst fears will not come about. The heightened anxiety will not kill you and does not mean you are insane. It's "just anxiety". That's what you need to label it. Just anxiety. Nothing more, nothing less.

The nature of anxiety is cyclical. It comes, it peaks, and it passes. When you feel the attack beginning, do not tell yourself horrible thoughts. That will create more of an adrenaline flow and will be like adding fuel to the fire. It's important to know that anxiety and relaxation are physiologically incompatible, which means that you can't be both at the same time. To the extent that you can produce any relaxation, you will begin to eliminate the anxiety.

So, at the earliest cues of the anxiety attack, tell yourself, "It's just anxiety. I've been through this before. It's uncomfortable but I can handle it. It will pass soon. This is an opportunity for me to learn how to produce relaxation. Let me concentrate on some deep diaphragmatic breathing. I needn't take seriously any disturbing thoughts. I'll let go of

41

them. They're just thoughts and I do not have to indulge them or be bluffed by them."

By focusing on your deep breathing and encouraging, realistic self-talk, you will be able to reverse the anxiety attacks quicker and quicker. A good therapist can help you understand the root causes of the anxiety and also help you to develop a repertoire of strategies and practical measures to deal more effectively with panic attacks.

Trungpa Rinpoche, a Tibetan Buddhist teacher, told the following story at a workshop I attended decades ago. The parentheses are my interpretations.

When Milarepa went back to his cave (mind), he was confronted with a gang of demons (disturbing thoughts). He tried everything he could to get rid of them. He read the Bible to them. He pleaded with them. He threatened them. He tried to hide from them. Milarepa was consumed by these demons. He tried to beat them away with a broom and exhausted himself in his frenzied attempts to get rid of them. Finally, he accepted that they were there and simply went about his business. At that point, slowly but surely, they began to let themselves out of his cave.

Waiting For Godot

What are you waiting for? For things to get better? For the right time? For someone to rescue you? Samuel Becket's *Waiting For Godot* is a simple yet complex play that has been subjected to many different interpretations over the years. It is a short play about two tramps who stand forever beside a road that leads to nowhere. The opening line of the play is, "Nothing to be done."

There is futility and an ultimate failure to do anything worthwhile. Each day is extremely tedious and time is seen as an inescapable burden. Amidst all of their confusion as to what to do, they never decisively act but only continue to wait for Godot. Lacking any meaning or enjoyment in their lives, they consider suicide but instead decide it would be better to simply wait for Godot. Shortly before the play's end, the two tramps agree they should go, but they do not move. The curtain comes down to end the play.

Godot has been interpreted as various things including God, a savior, happiness, or death. Regardless of the interpretation, the two men passively wait and wait and wait and are still waiting at the end of the play. They have chosen passivity. They do not see themselves as being responsible for the quality of their lives. It is hoped that Godot's arrival will change everything.

We want to feel better, more alive, and enjoy our lives, but sometimes we don't act decisively. We simply wish that our lives would be happier, more gratifying and stimulating. We generate interesting ideas and insights but rarely turn them into action. We procrastinate. We put off, delay, obsessively ruminate, or compulsively go about our day-to-day pedestrian existences that leave us at least a leap away from the fulfillment that we long for.

In essence, like the two main characters in the play, we wait for Godot. And wait. And wait. Zorba has said that the only real death is the death you die every day by not living fully.

Where There's a Will There's a Way

When my friend Carl was in high school, he set a goal for himself. He wanted to be a "Harvard Man". This was his dream. People who knew him thought it was more of a pipe dream, not considering Carl to be Harvard material, so to speak. He applied to a handful of colleges and although four accepted him, he was flatly rejected by Harvard. That however was not the end of his dream.

In college, Carl did well both academically and athletically. In fact, he developed into a nationally competitive sprinter for the track team. After a brilliant junior year, he applied to Harvard as a transfer student, this time believing that he had a great chance of being accepted. He didn't get in. Carl turned his focus toward graduate school and his dream of being a Harvard man continued. Harvard wasn't very concerned about his dream and rejected Carl for the third time. The dream seemingly had become not quite a nightmare, but something quite different than Carl originally had hoped for.

After college, job success, marriage, and a child, Carl found himself once again thinking of Harvard. Then it came to him like a bolt of lightening. Indeed, he would be a Harvard Man. He would donate his body to the Harvard Medical School. He sent a detailed letter explaining his almost life long interest in being a Harvard Man and how proud he would be to give his body to them. In the letter, he stated, "Instead of dying and going to heaven, I look forward to dying and going to Harvard!" Then while visiting a friend in the Boston area, he spent time walking on the Harvard campus talking to students and purchasing various Harvard paraphernalia. He even managed to sit in on a class and talk to the professor afterward. Nirvana.

About two weeks later the letter from Harvard Medical School arrived. It stated, "Please try a local medical school". Maybe it was destiny. Maybe Carl was just not supposed to be a Harvard Man. That final rejection took place about ten years ago. I'm happy to say that life went on for Carl. He's had an active fulfilling decade since his final rejection and is certainly not preoccupied with never having been accepted to Harvard.

So perhaps you really can find happiness despite important things not working out exactly as you hoped they would. Oh, I almost forgot to mention that Carl confided in me that in his will, he has asked his wife to cremate him and spread his ashes all over the great lawn at Harvard.

How Old Are You?

Satchel Paige was a great pitcher in the old Negro baseball league. Long before Jackie Robinson became the first black major leaguer in the late 1940's, Satchel Paige was a star. He was so good, that even at a very advanced age, he was able to make it to the major leagues.

Legend has it that although reporters continually questioned him as to his age, he never gave them a direct or satisfactory reply. He just went out there and pitched in the majors to batters that were old enough to be at least his sons and conceivably his grandsons. Reporters continued to ask his age. Finally, a bit exasperated, he turned to them one day and reportedly said, "How old would you be if you didn't know how old you was?"

Satchel Paige really did not know his age. He posed a wonderful question to the reporters. I'd like to ask the same question. How old would you be if you didn't know how old you were? We all know old 50 year olds and young 70 year olds. Birthdays with zeros on the end seem to have a big impact on us. Turning 30 or 40 or 50 or 60 may bring with it ways of thinking about yourself that influence your psyche and your soma. There is a big market for "Over-the-Hill" objects that are given to people on certain birthdays. Sadly, some of the recipients indeed feel over-the-hill.

When my friend Carl ran a 200 meter race at age 51 and was later interviewed by a cable TV program about why he was sprinting at this age, he stated, "We're redefining what it is to be fifty."

Sometimes I wonder whether it's a help or a hindrance to know your actual age. I don't think it's really that vital. Chronological age is not nearly as important as your spiritual age, or mind's age, or your heart's age. Take a cue from Satchel Paige.

Bodhidharma

I had grave doubts that I'd ever get to be a psychologist. It all hinged upon my understanding of a course called statistics. I didn't have a clue. I knew I wanted to be a clinical psychologist and help people feel better. Why there was a required course in statistics baffled me. How was that even remotely connected to what I wanted to do? During my undergraduate work, I dropped the course because I didn't want to fail it. I had to take it again and barely passed. At that same time I got a D in a general psychology course and felt discouraged. I persisted.

In graduate school while working on my Masters degree in psychology, I needed to pass a course called Advanced Statistics. I still had little to no understanding of the concepts and was absolutely thrilled to get out of that course with a C grade. I thought about going on for my Ph.D. and I thought about statistics. With trepidation, I went on.

In Utah, I was going for my doctorate when it became clear that this was a serious matter. I would have to pass a four-hour written examination in statistics. If by some miracle I was able to pass it, that would entitle me to take a four-hour oral examination with three of the most feared professors on campus. In my despair, I wrote to my parents in NJ and regretfully advised them that I may not be able to complete the requirements of the program. They told me to try hard. I stuck with it.

I became somewhat consumed with statistics. I asked for help from my fellow students. I sought out professors. I studied deep into the night and frequently all night. Statistics and I were strange bedfellows. Month after month, I kept trying to make sense out of this foreign language. Then something strange occurred. I would have never believed it. I began to understand statistics. And as my understanding grew, my excitement grew and I even began to like statistics. I persisted.

Bodhidharma is a famous fierce eyed Zen monk who in the 6th century A.D. came to China from India and brought with him a practical realism to Zen in contrast to the more scholastic and philosophical Buddhism that was dominant in China. Bodhidharma sat on Shoshitsu Mountain for nine years, meditating day and night. He became known far and wide for his unwavering determination.

When Bodhidharma resided at the temple of Shorin which was situated on Mount Su, a scholar named Eka sought his teachings. Bodhidharma continued meditating and spoke no word to the visitor. Three years later, Eka climbed the mountain again in mid-winter. Bodhidharma continued meditating and paid no attention to him. Eka stood in the snow all night. By morning, he was buried to his waist in snow drifts.

Bodhidharma acknowledged him. To prove his sincerity and determination to waken his Buddha nature, Eka drew his dagger, cut off his left arm, and presented it to Bodhidharma. This "cutting off" is not necessarily to be taken literally, but may be more symbolic in nature.

Both Eka and Bodhidharma persisted. They were determined. They went on difficult journeys. They hung in there. They handled crises. They endured. They gave it their all. Are you? You too can have fierce determination, courage, and heart. You too can proceed with passion.

Oh, by the way, I passed the four hour written exam in statistics. Months later, I survived the four hour oral grilling. Years later, I was teaching general psychology in the same university where I had taken it as a student and gotten a D.

<u>Ice Cream</u>

It may be sacrilegious to admit, but I wasn't particularly thrilled with the movie "Titanic". Unlike many other people I know, seeing it once was more than enough. I understand that in this instance, mine is a minority opinion. I guess that's why they make vanilla and chocolate (and at least thirty seven other flavors of ice cream). As I stood looking at a painting years ago, I remember a person walking by saying, "Who would ever buy that?". I did.

Now, I understand that I'm talking about trivial things, but people can take trivial things quite seriously and argue vehemently about them. When people disagree, things that are not so trivial can become stumbling blocks that interfere with relationships. The point I'd like to make is it is okay for people to disagree, to have their own opinions, likes and dislikes.

When these differences occur, try not to get caught up in power struggles in which you have to win or convince the other person that his position is inferior. Stop thinking in terms of black or white, correct or incorrect. In most situations, it won't matter a great deal whether you do it your way or his way. Both the scenic route and the direct route will get you to your destination. They're just different routes, not necessarily better or worse.

Arguments don't need to be settled by a judge or jury. I didn't like "Titanic". You probably did. That's fine. I may put the toilet paper roll on so that you pull from the bottom and you may do it the opposite way. You may vote Republican. I might not. You may be convinced about the need for capital punishment. I may be less certain. We can still be neighbors, co-workers, friends, or lovers who respect each other and go to dinner together. After dinner and some lively discussion, we'll stop for ice cream. You'll order chocolate and I'll get vanilla.

Free At Last

When we start attending more consciously to our freedom of choice, things begin to get interesting. I think it is fair to say that with the concept of freedom of choice, the plot thickens. If we are free to choose what we want to do, think and feel, then why don't we feel good? It has been postulated that people truly don't want the kind of freedom I'm suggesting we have. It may be experienced as too much of a burden to have that kind of responsibility rest squarely on your shoulders – the burden of knowing that you are responsible for your emotional state. Yet, the acceptance of that responsibility can change your life. I'll try to clarify this by discussing the so called "death of God" that philosophers such as Nietzsche and Sartre wrote about.

An Interview With God

Interviewer: I am rather surprised to be here with you. I'm sure you have heard the rumor that you are dead.

God: Heard it? I started it. I needed some time off. Do you have any idea how tiring it is listening to complaints and demands all day? And the amount of junk mail I get is outrageous.

I: So you decided to get away from it all.

G: That's right. I went incognito to Argentina, but a rumor started circulating that I was hiding there. It wasn't long before the telemarketers caught up with me.

I: What do you have in store for the world? What are you going to create next?

G: You have a short attention span. I'm unemployed. Let people create their own world. They can believe in me but they shouldn't rely upon me to solve all their day to day problems. And please don't tell anyone I'm alive and well and thinking about collecting unemployment.

I: Well, okay. I guess no one would believe me anyhow.

G: You're right. You'd probably end up in a mental hospital getting Thorazine for breakfast. Hey, what do you say we grab a bite of lunch?

I: Yeah, I'm starved. God, that's a great idea!

Entertaining the death of God has nothing to do with atheism, per se, or even theism. The death of God is a metaphor dealing with the pain of independence and freedom. If the creator is gone from heaven, creators must be found on earth. Therefore, it is up to you to be creative in carving out a meaningful existence for yourself. This places a heavy burden on the individual and it's been postulated that this relates to the significance of Nietzsche's having a madman witness the death of God.

A madman refers to a person who behaves in a crazy manner, and a madman also refers to an enraged person. So the metaphorical death of God may place a heavy burden on you, but it may also set you free. If indeed it is you that is responsible for your misery or dissatisfaction, you are in a position to do something about it.

Johnny Drew a Monster

A little boy once drew a four panel cartoon for me. The 1st panel showed a boy drawing and was captioned "Johnny drew a monster". The 2nd panel showed a boy running scared. It was captioned "The monster chased him". Panel #3 showed a scary creature closing in on the running boy. The caption was "Just in time...". The final panel showed only about 1/3 of the monster, and was captioned, "Johnny erased him". So we have:

> Johnny drew a monster,
> The monster chased him.
> Just in time...
> Johnny erased him.

Although the boy told me that he had made that poem up, decades later I discovered it was originally composed by the noted author Lilian Moore. Without realizing it, much of the time, we create monsters that haunt and taunt us. We can all be Dr. Frankensteins.

Once, a man came to me very agitated and dismayed. He explained that he couldn't sleep at night unless he counted from 1 through 8, and then counted backwards from 8 through 1. He felt abnormal and was not sleeping much at all. He asked what he should do. I immediately responded that when he goes to bed, he should count from 1 to 8 and then from 8 to 1 and then go to sleep. He was amazed that I wasn't terribly concerned, but he took my advice. Years later when I saw him at a gathering and asked how he was sleeping, he replied, "Better than ever!"

Many of the things that bother us are our own creations. If we are able to see that clearly, we can begin to de-create the monsters or at the very least turn them into friendly ghosts.

<u>Take It Easy</u>

I have a message that I want you to get. Slow down. That's it. That's the message. I have noticed that in essence, I'm a different person when I'm not in a hurry. I take more time to talk to people, drive a bit slower, take a little more in then I usually do and hum a pinch more. I won't race to get into the post office before the person coming from the opposite direction and I won't tailgate or curse at the driver in front of me. I'll spend a little bit more time with people on the phone without feeling harried or put upon. All this seems to happen when I'm not pressed for time.

Studies have been done in the field of social psychology to get at this phenomenon. Researchers have enlisted the help of actors to simply lay on the ground as if they had passed out or were hurt. In large cities during the morning rush to get to work, a very high percentage of pedestrians walk right by or over the person lying on the sidewalk without stopping to assist the person or assess the situation more closely.

The percentage of people stopping to help increases in non-rush hours and it also increases in suburban areas where life may be a little less hurried. It seems we are all somewhat nicer and more concerned when we are not rushing around. Yet, many of us create such busy lifestyles with non-stop agendas that it's almost as if we don't have the time to feel as good as we can or be as nice as we're capable of being. Try to slow down a little and take things as they come.

I'm reminded of the story of a man who puts on a coat that he hasn't worn in three years. In the pocket he finds a shoe repair ticket. He goes to the shoemaker and silently presents him with the old ticket. The shoemaker takes the ticket with him into the back of the store and emerges a few minutes later. Handing the ticket back to the man, the shoemaker calmly said, "They'll be ready Tuesday."

The Heart of the Matter

I find it meaningful to think of the 'heart' as representing the essence or vital core of a person – the seat of the emotions. Many people have "lost heart" or have become discouraged. Some are "eating their hearts out" or are consumed by remorse or grief. Others have suffered deep disappointments and disillusionments – the "heartsick". People have little "heartaches" and major "heartbreaks". Some become "heartless" or withdrawn and apathetic, while others are chronically angry or "cruel hearted".

R.D. Laing, in his book The Politics of Experience, recognized that some schizophrenics may be better described as having broken (schiz) hearts (phrenos), rather than split (schiz) personalities (phrenos). The schizophrenic person may indeed be the brokenhearted, while the classical neurotic diagnosis might be reserved for the person with the wounded heart who tries to defend against further dispiriting events.

I find the research on death from all causes in general, and heart disease specifically, to be very enlightening. To feel loved or connected is in fact lifesaving. People who feel disconnected (lonely, isolated, depressed) have three to five times greater rates of death and disease than those with a sense of being connected (a sense of belongingness, community, intimacy). So, in fact, there may be a strong correlation between physical well-being and emotional well-being.

Remember how the tin man got his heart. It really wasn't from the wizard. He got connected. His support from the lion, Dorothy, and the scarecrow, and his reciprocating that support were key determinants in his being successful in his quest. He learned to believe in himself and take risks that enabled him to get his heart.

A good formula for health is to be "good hearted" and get connected. And that's the heart of the matter.

Take a Mid-Week Break

When I was a kid, it was difficult to find a doctor on a Wednesday. For some strange reason, their offices were closed. When I got a bit older, I asked a doctor about this. He explained to me that stress is a killer, literally and figuratively. He believed stress was a major contributor to the ailments that brought about 75% of the patients to his office. As I wondered what this had to do with my question, he finally delivered the explanation.

If you took Wednesday off, you would most likely never work more than 3 consecutive days. Because the effects of stress are cumulative (remember the proverbial straw that broke the camel's back), taking that mid-week day off insured that you had an opportunity to de-stress, assuming that your job is a stressful one. He went on to say that it's the fourth consecutive work day that adds significant stress, and that the fifth straight work day "is the killer".

I realize that not everyone is in the position to be able to take Wednesday off. If you can't, can you modify it? Is it possible to take a half-day off? Or, how about simply doing whatever you can to lighten the load on Wednesdays, like scheduling fewer appointments, delegating certain tasks or allowing yourself more time to complete what's necessary to do. If you are unable to incorporate any of the above ideas for Wednesdays, perhaps you can at least talk to yourself in a relaxing way and make sure you use your breaks to unwind.

Can you take a ten minute walk, or sit quietly and breathe deeply for a few minutes?

Wednesday turns out to be an important day for your mental and physical well-being. Honor it by doing what you can to restore yourself. Treat yourself nicely all the time, but treat yourself especially well on Wednesday.

Dealing With Loss

Mostly all of us have had to deal with the death of a loved one. There is no substitute for a supportive network of family and friends as well as the passage of time. How much time is difficult to say. So called "normal grieving" can be months or years. There is a huge range of individual variability. Do not expect others will grieve similarly to you. For example, if a mother dies, her five children may all grieve quite differently. One or two siblings may need a much longer time frame to deal with the loss than do the other siblings.

I have found that the year following a loved one's death is generally the most difficult one for the griever. Going through the first set of holidays, birthdays, anniversaries, and other landmark dates can be dreadful. That first mother's day after her death or the first Thanksgiving without her can be brutal. In time, we find the wherewithal to go on in meaningful ways and celebrate holidays and enjoy life.

As a therapist, I occasionally help people with the grieving process. They have to be ready and willing to do this. I'll explain the procedure to them first, and take them through it if they want to. Some people choose not to. The ones who choose to participate almost always feel better for having done so. It's called "empty chair" work and is rooted in Perl's Gestalt psychotherapy. I recently worked with a woman named Carol whose mother had died of an unexpected illness about nine months before we engaged in this work together. I put an empty chair before her and said,

"Carol, imagine vividly that your mother is sitting here before you. Picture her clearly. I want you to talk directly to her. Don't talk about her to me or talk in the third person. Talk to her. Start by telling her your regrets."

When Carol finished telling her mother of her regrets, I had her get up and move to the empty chair. I said,

"Carol. Now I want you to take the role of your mother. Become her and speak to Carol" (now represented by the other empty chair, the one Carol was originally sitting on).

When her mother was finished speaking, I had Carol return to her original chair and once again speak to her mother. Carol engaged in the switching of chairs numerous times. I gave her the opportunity to speak to her mother about anything, but also specifically asked her to tell her mother of her resentments and appreciations. Carol's mother always had the opportunity to speak after hearing what Carol had to say. When it was appropriate, I had Carol and her mother say their goodbyes to each other.

To participate in the empty chair work is an extremely draining process. I've always helped people through it rather than ask them to do it by themselves. I think that grieving a loved one can be one of the most difficult things we do in life. Be patient. Be accepting of all your feelings. Let time pass.

Metaphorical Reincarnation

Who you were yesterday need have very little bearing on who you are today or who you will be tomorrow. It is natural to evolve, to grow, to be born again. The non-literal or metaphorical view or reincarnation suggests that you can have many incarnations in this lifetime. You are not a static entity. Even if you have had a long period of stagnation or dormancy, you are still capable of changing, or re-inventing yourself. If you insist that you cannot change, that you cannot be different, you are clinging to a false belief. You are denying your freedom and are not in touch with your power and potential.

I have a vested interest in metaphorical reincarnation. That's because I'm a psychologist and I've worked with thousands of people who have been stuck in incarnations that were troubling. My job is to help get them unstuck and able to re-invent themselves.

As a therapist, I firmly believe that people can, in essence, reincarnate in this lifetime. I have seen it again and again. Sometimes therapy is kind of like an argument in which the person insists she cannot change and I insist she can (because I know that to be the case). This argument can go on for quite a while and can be very emotionally draining, but it's always done in an atmosphere of caring and respect. She tells me she can't reincarnate . I tell her that she can. We repeat this dance again and again in a myriad of forms. I give it my all. I want so badly to win the argument. I realize that if she wins, she loses.

Free At Last [Reprisal]

It is an understatement to say that it is difficult to accept responsibility for your emotional well-being or the lack of it. Yet it is crucial that you fully get the message that your misery or happiness is determined by you. To that aim, I would like to tell you about Victor Frankl and also paraphrase Camus' "The Myth of Sisyphus".

The noted psychiatrist, Dr. Victor Frankl, wrote about his experiences in Nazi death camps. For three years he was confined against his will and experienced daily atrocities. During this time, his father, mother, brother, wife, and friends died in the camps. Hunger, torture, and brutality were everyday occurrences. There was no escape.

Yet, Frankl considered himself to be free during the entire ordeal. His captors could not take away from him the power to decide on how he was going to let the circumstances he found himself in affect him. He recognized his choices and took responsibility for them. He did not choose to give up hope. He didn't choose to wither away and die. He chose thoughts, actions, and feelings that enabled him to live in those circumstances as best he could. He chose to believe the horrors would end and that he would be able to develop new meaningful relationships and live a full life. He believed that you could never take away a person's freedom to choose one's attitude in any set of circumstances.

Camus tells us that because Sisyphus had angered the gods, he was condemned to ceaselessly roll a huge rock up to the mountain top. It required every ounce of his being to do so. As soon as he would reach the top, the rock would fall back to the bottom of the mountain. This was his eternal task. Supposedly, if you look closely enough, you can see a wry smile on Sisyphus' face. Although he always finds his burden again and again, he is still master of his own fate. He has decided to make the struggle itself a worthwhile experience. Only he can decide how he will approach the task he finds for himself. Sisyphus is free.

The Yogi and the Fork Bender

I would categorize myself as a down to earth guy. I prefer realism to science fiction. I'm not exactly a "show me, I'm from Missouri" kind of guy, but I'm close. Fame and fortune and magic don't impress me.

There is the story of the king who promised a Yogi the best horse in the kingdom if he could go into a trance and stay buried alive for a year. So they buried the Yogi, but in the course of the year the kingdom was overthrown and nobody remembered to dig up the powerful Yogi. Twenty years later, someone came across the Yogi who was still in his deep trance. After he was woken up, the first thing the Yogi said was, "Where is my horse?"

Years ago, there was a guy on television who seemed to be able to bend forks simply by using his mind. My only thought on the matter was that if he had that kind of power, couldn't he do something useful or helpful or therapeutic. The powers of the horse seeking Yogi and the fork-bending T.V. personality are interesting, but that's about it. To me, these "miracles" pale in comparison to ordinary day to day actions that help make this a better world.

I think the mother who reassures her daughter or makes her son a bowl of soup when they're not feeling well is powerful. Her actions make a difference. How about the ordinary firefighters and police who responded such as they did to the events of September 11, 2001.

You can make an extraordinary difference. Remember the Jimmy Stewart character in the movie It's a Wonderful Life (rent it if by some remote chance you're never seen it). Think of the scenes that showed what others' lives would have been like if he had actually never existed. Now, think about your own life and the impact you've had on others, maybe without ever acknowledging it. Just wake up, live fully, take care of yourself (in all ways) and your loved ones, and be a decent person. That should do it. You don't need to be a Yogi or a Fork Bender.

R and R

In the army, following a difficult tour of duty, you some-times were able to get a few days of what was termed R and R (rest and recreation). This was immensely helpful in feeling restored and therefore feeling ready to resume another hard assignment. I think we all could benefit from R and R at least once every few months.

One of my favorites is to spend a rainy Sunday in bed. It starts with my wife and I sleeping a little later than usual, followed by breakfast in bed. I'll usually make it and bring it up to the bedroom, although on rare occasions we'll sleep out and order room service. Then, with absolutely nothing on the agenda and the T.V. off, we'll curl up with the Sunday papers (the NY Times helps) for a couple of hours. If we're really feeling decadent, we'll nap for an hour, do a crossword, watch a video, or find some way to pass the whole afternoon without ever leaving the bedroom except to bring up something to eat.

I think you should design your own R and R. Whatev-er works for you that is restful, destressing, and leaves you energized and feeling good. It doesn't matter how my R and R sounds to you or how your R and R sounds to me. What mat-ters is that you take the time to do whatever it is that restores you.

Life can be very draining. Stress is cumulative. It builds and builds and may lead to the development of symptoms. Because stress is cumulative, it becomes essential to find avenues that alleviate stress. Look for early warning signs that you are becoming overly stressed. A red light should come on if you are any of the following:

*less tolerant
*unable to sleep normally
*more easily agitated
*having crying spells
*uninterested in socializing
*manifesting an appetite disturbance
*startled more easily than usual
*having night sweats
*lacking concentration
*forgetting many things
*excessively nervous
*having palpitations
*trembling
*dizzy or lightheaded
*fearing losing control
*fearing going crazy
*experiencing lots of muscle tension
*depressed
*feeling numb
*unable to think clearly
*abusing alcohol and/or other drugs

The red light serves the purpose of getting you to see that if you don't do something to help yourself, you may develop further symptoms and risk a serious emotional disturbance. There are many ways to destress including counseling, yoga, meditation, exercise, time off, re-inventing yourself and your relationships, restructuring your work schedule, confiding in a friend, taking part in a support group, and on and on.

If the red light comes on, pay attention, and create an R and R that feels right to you. As you know, if you continue to disregard red lights and go right through them, it's only a matter of time before you pay the consequences.

May the Force Be With You

Take five or ten minutes each day to express your gratitude. Instead of focusing on problems, disappointments, or frustrations, think of everything you can be grateful for. To begin with, you've been given another day of life. That's a good starting point.

We all take millions of things for granted everyday. For example, that we can see, hear, smell, walk, talk, and so on. Express your gratitude silently to yourself and make some kind of cosmic connection that has meaning for you. It doesn't matter whether you express your gratitude to God, Buddha, Christ, or Allah. Or whether it's to Nature, Jehovah, The Force, Energy, the Universe, or any other higher power.

Expressing gratitude is a way of appreciating life and is a very healthy and healing activity. I'm convinced that on a physiological level, there's biochemistry produced that is unique unto itself. I believe expressing gratitude produces beneficial brain wave patterns and an enhanced immune system functioning. It has psychological correlates as well, as it helps you feel a sense of belongingness and significance.

Write a list of all the things you're grateful for. It can be a general list (i.e., "my health") or a very detailed list (i.e., "my toes, my feet, my legs, my fingers, my hands, my arms, my immune system, my…"). The general list may include the listing "friends". The detailed list might include "Dennis, Joyce,

Beth, Sal, Karen, Sherry, Tony, Joe…". Look at the list and ab-sorb it. Seeing it in black and white is sometimes helpful.

Much of the time we think or pray about things that we're troubled by and forget to think of the many wondrous things in life that we simply take for granted. So, take five – for expressing your gratitude.

<u>Yadda Yadda Yadda</u>

Do you make New Year's resolutions? Most surveys find that typically, those well-meaning resolutions are broken within hours or days. I have a brother who quit smoking New Year's Day for 25 consecutive years. There are a lot of people who don't make resolutions because they realize the vast majority of them don't come to fruition. Not a very optimistic outlook. I'm not sure if I have a preference between making resolutions and not keeping them, or not making them at all.

I do know that good intentions aren't enough in and of themselves. It's very easy to talk a good game, but words don't necessarily reflect reality. How many husbands, wives, or lovers have assured their partners how much they love them while their actions belie their words?

It's not unusual for there to be a marked discrepancy between what a person says and what a person does. Put your faith in the actions, not the words. The truth is more likely reflected in behaviors than in verbalizations. That's why I'll continually assess my actions. The proof is in the pudding (I have no idea where that expression came from).

I won't make resolutions, but I'll tell myself to <u>do</u> specific things. It's not enough to generally resolve, "I'm going to be nicer to my wife". Instead, I'll do at least two things each day that demonstrate this. For example, I'll (a) call her at work just to say I'm thinking about her and miss her, and (b) give her a foot massage tonight. Instead of saying "I'm going to get

77

in better shape this year," do at least two things each day to demonstrate this. You can (a) walk each morning for a half hour, and (b) use light dumbbells during every television commercial.

Rather than pay the general lip service to losing weight as a resolution, just do at least two things daily demonstrating this such as (a) eating fruits and vegetables, and (b) eating baked potatoes topped with seasonings rather than indulging that desire for french fries. You get the idea. Watch the behaviors to get at what's really going on with you or with anybody else. There's no truth except in action.

The Gift of Giving

It was the morning of my birthday and I was feeling good. I felt grateful to be alive. I reflected upon those who weren't as fortunate (friends and family members who died young). It struck me that I felt more like giving than receiving. Knowing that there would be a small family birthday celebration that night, I decided that I would surprise all those in attendance by buying each one of them a small but heartfelt gift. Thinking about each of them as unique individuals, I was able to get interesting little gifts for my wife, daughter, son, sister-in-law, brother-in-law, and niece.

That night, when I brought out the gifts for everyone, they didn't know quite what to make of it. I was happy to be able to share my birthday with them and wanted them to know it. My giving gifts to them on my birthday certainly gave rise to jokes about my mental health, being backwards, and so on.

That was 15 years ago. I have given gifts on my birthday to others every year since then. Sometimes, the people in attendance change, although the same nucleus is usually there. There may be a friend of mine or one of the other family members. It doesn't change things. I don't mind at all that I need to pick up an extra gift or two. I never tell anyone that "I gave at the office". I like the idea of giving. It's something we can all get better at. Giving of our time. Manifesting a generosity of spirit.

79

I like to throw coins into the salvation army pot during the holiday season. It's fun to buy lemonade from 2 little kids setting up shop on a neighborhood corner. Holding doors open, saying something nice to someone, smiling, really giving somebody your undivided attention, greeting someone with a firm handshake while looking them straight in the eye, letting someone go ahead of you in line – there are lots of little ways to be giving. You can even buy someone else a gift on your birthday!

On Hawaii, Alaska, and the 47 Contiguous States

Every year, my wife and myself and our son and daughter take a summer vacation inCape Cod. Twelve years ago, when the kids were 10 (they're twins), we began playing a game during the 4 ½ hour car trip from New Jersey to the Cape. We tried to see how many states we could find license plates for. Our goal was to eventually get all fifty states even if it took us a long time. We're still playing.

Although we now have four drivers in the family looking and looking, one state still eludes us. Can you guess which license plate we've never seen? Surprisingly enough, we've gotten both Hawaii and Alaska at least five or six times. Idaho, Nebraska, Kansas, and Oregon have all succumbed. Delaware and Rhode Island were no problem at all. The two Washingtons (state and D.C.) were a breeze. The no-show is North Dakota.

Not once in twelve years has a North Dakota license plate appeared. Last year, we even briefly considered vacationing to North Dakota so as to finally reach a resolution to our twelve-year itch. Sane heads prevailed as we quickly ruled out that possibility. We thought about writing or calling people in North Dakota and having them send old plates or at least a picture of their license plates. We decided to wait it out and play fair and square.

I'm a patient person and recognize that things sometimes happen for a reason. Keeping in mind the old Ecclesiastes line that "there's a time for everything under the sun", I figured that we didn't need to do anything dramatic and when the time is right we could discover that elusive license plate.

Yesterday, I was sitting at a traffic light in our home town and suddenly got a very intense, almost bordering on the mystical, sensation that the van pulling next to me at the light was from North Dakota. I would let it pull away first when the light changed green so that I could get a good look at it. Finally, it pulled out and I got a look at the plate. And there it was…a New Jersey plate. Not exactly the kind of miracle I'd been looking for, but it did put a smile on my face as I thought of the Zen teaching of finding the miraculous in the ordinary.

The ordinary, the pedestrian, the typical day to day sights and sounds that we take for granted. A New Jersey plate right here in New Jersey. Of course! Will miracles never cease. I guess if we had found North Dakota years ago when we found every other state and plates from Guam, Nova Scotia, and seemingly half the world, I would have never written this story. And by the way, if you can mail me an old license plate from North Dakota, I'd appreciate it.

Looking In the Mirror

Over forty years ago I was able to begin my college education because of deferred low-interest college loans. I was the youngest of six children. None of my older siblings had gone to college. My parents did not have the money to pay for my education. I was pretty much left to my own devices. If I wanted to go to college, I'd have to find one and pay for it.

I applied to one school and was accepted. Then, I borrowed as much money as I could to finance my undergraduate studies. I think the maximum was ten thousand dollars. That went a long way back then. The way the New Jersey Higher Education Loan Program was set up, I didn't have to begin repaying the loan until I finished school, and then had ten years to repay it.

I began to faithfully send in my monthly payments. It was very surprising to me when I learned that many, many people were defaulting on these student loans. There were newspaper articles and segments on television news shows that brought this to light. Friends kidded me that I was one of the few who was actually repaying a student loan. It never entered my mind to do anything other than repay the loan. If it hadn't been for that loan, I wouldn't have been able to attend college. I was thankful for that loan program and didn't mind paying it off at all. And besides that, when you get up every morning, you have to look at yourself in the mirror.

Make choices that you can live with, that don't compromise your values. Don't do what the majority does if it doesn't feel right to you. If it feels wrong to you, it probably is, no matter what rationalizations you tell yourself.

In a small village a hundred years ago, a father gave each of his two young daughters a live chicken. He said to them, "Take the chicken where no one can see and kill it and bring it back here." The one daughter returned in fifteen minutes with the dead chicken. The other daughter returned an hour later with her live chicken. When the father asked what happened, the daughter said, "Wherever I went, the chicken saw and I saw."

The Land of Fools

When we live or work in close quarters with others day in and day out, it may become necessary at times to amend, modify, correct, or respond to other people's comments and behaviors. Sometimes we might have to send them a difficult message. Messages that could be disturbing to get may be received better if they come from a caring messenger. When you deal with your husband or lover, your child, your parent, your co-worker, your neighbor, or the clerk at the store, don't only focus on the message that needs to be sent, but consider how best to get that message across.

Words are very powerful, and once uttered, can never be taken back. They can cause wounds that last a lifetime. Aside from the actual verbalizations, your intonations and attitude speak volumes, as do your non-verbal communications (i.e., shrugs, head shaking, frowns, stares, gestures, and so on).

Once upon a time, there was a man who happened to come upon a place known as the Land of Fools. He soon saw a number of people fleeing in terror from a field. They said to him, "There is a monster in that field!" He looked and saw that it was a watermelon.

He offered to kill the "monster" for them. After he cut the melon from its stalk, he sliced it up and began to eat it. The people became even more terrified of him than they had been of the melon. Driving him away with pitchforks, they cried, "He will kill us next unless we get rid of him."

Years later, a woman stumbled upon the Land of Fools, and the same events began to happen. But, instead of killing the "monster", she tiptoed away from it with them. She spent time with them in their houses and gained their confidence. Little by little, she taught them the basic facts about watermelon that would enable them not only to lose their fear of melons but even to cultivate them themselves.

The Frightened Child

There may be a part of you that wants to make changes. That part of you envisions doing things differently and becoming a happier person. The problem is that there may be a part of you that is resistant to going along with your game plan. This part of you will give you messages to the effect of "you can't", or "you shouldn't...". This part of you may sabotage the part of you that wants to go forward, grow, and evolve.

The part of you that says you don't deserve it or you don't have what it takes is what I refer to as the frightened child within you. Expecting to be criticized or to fail, the frightened child within you will opt for not venturing into unchartered waters. Believing that you're not smart enough, good enough, or attractive enough, that part of you will either consciously or sub-consciously take the starch out of your ideas related to making changes that involve your taking a chance on yourself.

Think about the watermelon story you just read about. You need to apply it to yourself. To begin with, learn to recognize when the frightened child's voice is talking to you and label it as such. Then you need to patiently nurture that child by talking to her in a reasonable, reassuring, and comforting way.

In other words, the more rational adult voice within you needs to take center stage and talk to the frightened child to help her get unstuck – to help her gain confidence and believe in herself. You can talk to the frightened child so that over the course of time she will become more playful and less anxious. She can learn to let go of her fears and take it all a bit less seriously. Remember, it starts with recognizing her voice and labeling it as the frightened child. Then, embrace her and slowly but surely teach her that it's okay and she's okay and that it's only a watermelon.

A Funny Thing Happened on the Way to the Forum

My friend Donna was a government lawyer for years prior to her first pregnancy. Eagerly looking forward to the arrival of her child, she already felt strong maternal instincts. She balked when her agency offered her an eight-week maternity leave. She wanted one year. The good lawyer that she was, Donna passionately and persistently negotiated a plan that was to her liking.

Although her employer was not thrilled, it was agreed that Donna would take six months of total leave, followed by two months of working one day a week, followed by two months of working two days weekly, followed by two months of working three days each week. After that one-year period, she was scheduled to return to work full-time. She had labored long and hard to pull off the above timetable and felt confident this would enable her to bond with and nurture her child to her satisfaction.

Donna had a healthy baby daughter and was ecstatic. She settled into motherhood and things went very well. That is, for about eight weeks. Although Donna loved her daughter dearly, she began to feel restless and increasingly missed work and everything that came along with it. She called her boss and asked if she could re-negotiate her maternity leave plan.

Three months after her daughter's birth, Donna was back at work full-time. She was satisfied with the child care arrangements she had worked out, and although she had some mixed feelings about her full time return to work, Donna realized this was the way for her to go. She was more surprised than anyone about this turn of events.

Sometimes we have fantasies of how things will be. The reality at times is very different than the fantasy. Sometimes we have to make important decisions based upon insufficient experiential information. Donna was wise enough not to stick to her preconceived game plan when it became evident to her that she miscalculated with regard to her maternity leave. She didn't need twelve months leave, she only needed three. Her decision to re-think her original decision and act accordingly may have saved her nine months of dissatisfaction. When I think of the old proverb, "A stitch in time saves nine", I think of Donna.

Pay Attention

Most of the important lessons in life are not taught in the classroom. In fact, when I've lectured to classes and waxed poetically, deeming myself brilliant, students fell asleep with regularity. When I share life experiences with them, at least some of them are on the edge of their seats (well, they're awake anyhow). We are always in the midst of teachings but tend not to recognize them. If we carefully observe nature, animals, people, and events, teachings will come forth readily.

If you think you've already learned all of life's important lessons, you may be shutting down your potential to enrich your life. There's a saying that, "If a pick-pocket meets a holy-man, he'll only see his pockets". I thought I knew it all when I was 30. By 40, I realized I still had a lot to learn. At 50, I was less smug than ever and ready to see just about everything as a potential lesson.

It's been said that when the student is ready, the teacher appears. Always be ready. The teachings will come and you will grow as a result. Learn from frustration and disappointment. Learn from your achievements, crises, and blessings. Watch nature carefully. The small trees whose branches, heavy by winter's snow, bend but do not break. The cow giving birth while four or five other cows help her clean the afterbirth from the newborn calf. The wisdom of the changing of the seasons. Watch infants and the aged. From cradle to grave there are sermons all around us.

There is the story of a father and his young son driving along and they suddenly have to stop at a train crossing. The father frowns and says, "Oh, no, we have to wait for the damned train." And the son says, "Oh, boy, we get to watch the train go by." Pay attention.

Trust Yourself

Riding home from Cape Cod in the early morning hours of August, 2003, I discovered I was in the midst of a classic sign of our times. I was surrounded by sports utility vehicles (SUV's). I jokingly said to my son that cars are becoming extinct and that the next 10 vehicles to pass us would either be SUV's, vans, or pick-up trucks. I was wrong. The next 13 were. It's hard to throw a stone without hitting an SUV.

Recently, there was considerable pressure on me to join the parade. My old Subaru was on its last legs and it was time to purchase something new. My wife opted for an SUV. The kids also thought that was a great idea. I wasn't quite so certain but decided to consider the idea. I test-drove several of them. I researched them. I watched the news magazine show segments on them.

Frankly, I didn't quite understand what all the fuss was about. Since I had no plans to drive across the Baja Peninsula or didn't feel the need to sit high in the saddle, I considered factors like gas mileage, comfort, cost, and the like. I don't mean to knock SUV's and I'm aware there's a high likelihood that you own one. It just wasn't right for me. They are a hot item and getting hotter. Maybe one day I'll see the light, but for now I'm going to trust my own judgment.

Years ago there was a psychology experiment in which groups of nine people were shown one card (the standard card) which had a line drawn on it. They were then shown another card (the comparison card) that had 3 lines drawn on it, one of the lines matching exactly the length of the line on the other card. They viewed the two cards simultaneously and were asked to indicate which line on the comparison card was the same length as the line on the standard card.

The lines were different enough that under ordinary circumstances, mistakes would be made less than one percent of the time. However, this experiment was not conducted under ordinary circumstances, because all but one of the members of each group were instructed beforehand to unanimously agree on incorrect answers. In other words, in each group of 9 people, 8 of them were in cahoots (collusion) with the experimenter. All eight would offer the same answer as being correct although it was clearly not so. Then, the ninth person (the only one truly being tested) would have to answer. The startling results showed that only about a fourth of the subjects did not yield to the pressures of the group. The others conformed.

Anyhow, I did purchase a new vehicle. It turned out to be an old fashioned car, a four-door sedan. I did go for a pinstripe and a moon-roof and a one disc CD player. I'm happy with it.

All of this is by way of suggesting that you are a unique person and should trust your judgment, even if at times it doesn't quite match the prevailing societal forces and opinions acting upon you. There is no other you in this entire universe. Be yourself. That is more than good enough.

The Garage Sale

Many years ago there was a movie (I don't remember the name) in which a panicked bride-to-be locked herself in the bathroom on the day of her wedding and would not come out. Her father tried everything he could think of to calm her fears and quell her anxiety. For a long time he spoke to her in a gentle, reassuring manner. Nothing worked. He begged and pleaded to no avail. He set up a long ladder outside the house and tried to climb in through the bathroom window. When all had failed and time was running short, the prospective groom was told about the situation. He boldly walked to the bathroom door, called his fiancée's name and yelled, "Cool it!" She opened the door and came out.

Have you ever had an experience where a few well-chosen words or a simple act by someone made all the difference? In that moment, you may have gotten unstuck or felt some kind of awakening.

My sister, Harriet, was recently dealing with a situation that was taking its toll on her. She had what she described as a "nightmare week". She felt down and out, and the situation was still unresolved. In an attempt to "start resembling a human being again", she went to a local garage sale. Being a collector of hard cover novels she quickly went to a pile of books. They were marked two-dollars each. Being in an ornery mood, my sister barked, "Hard cover books are usually one dollar at garage sales".

95

The man re-affirmed the two-dollar price, and added, "Here's one you might like". He handed her an Ann Rice novel. It was the only one she didn't have at home in the hard cover version. Thinking this was quite a coincidence, since Ann Rice was her favorite author, she paid the two dollars and left the garage sale. A minute later, for some unknown reason, she flipped through the pages of the book. In it, there was a bookmark with a handwritten message on it. It said, "LET GO, LET GOD."

My sister, who's not a particularly religious sort, was deeply affected by this and it enabled her to get a different perspective on the things that were bothering her. If you permit me some leeway in the use of the word, this was a "holy" moment for her. Whether you believe in God or are an atheist is not the issue. One of J.D. Salinger's characters (I think it was Seymour Glass) paraphrased the ancient Zen teaching to the effect that all we ever do in life is go from one piece of holy ground to the next. Be open to all your experiences. You may find your answer in the church sermon but you may be just as likely to find it at the garage sale.

No Thank You

Jewish mothers are stereotyped as being experts on creating guilt. There's the story of the young man whose mother gave him 2 shirts for his birthday. He was wearing one the next time he saw her and he said, "Hey mom, this shirt is great. Thanks a lot." She quickly replied, "What's the matter? You didn't like the other one?"

It's not only Jewish mothers that have a corner on the guilt market. Guilt is one of the primary tools used by parents and authority figures throughout the world in hopes of controlling children's behavior. Making someone feel guilty about their thoughts, feelings, or actions may get them to grasp what we consider as good or bad, right or wrong, acceptable or unacceptable. This is how the evolving child develops a sense of conscience. If parents are overly critical, the child may grow into an adult who manifests a harsh sense of conscience, therefore feeling too guilty too easily.

Guilt is a very strong emotion. If there is an ongoing sense of it, for example if you feel guilty that you never really met your parents' expectations of you, you may have a lurking sense of unhappiness or unworthiness. You may put yourself in self-defeating situations because of a less than conscious feeling that you don't deserve happiness or that you deserve to be punished for your shortcomings or wrongdoings.

Think about how you've been conditioned to accept invitations to feel guilty. Think about who has sent and who continues to send you these invitations. From now on, when anyone offers you an invitation to feel guilty, instead of automatically reaching for it, see it for what it is and say to yourself, "No, thank you." Assure yourself that you did nothing terrible and that you can't please all of the people, all of the time, and that that is okay.

As your guilt decreases, you'll have more energy to invest in positive thoughts and activities. Do not tell yourself that you're not good enough or that you're not worthwhile or loveable. Be on your side. It's been said, "If not you, who? If not now, when?".

<u>Buddha</u>

He was neither divine nor a savior, but simply an ordinary human being. Born Gautama Siddhartha approximately 2600 years ago, he was the son of a wealthy overprotective father. He lead a very sheltered childhood and adolescence. As he became a young man, he ventured into the real world and encountered an old person, a sick person, and a dead person, and he then realized that nothing lasts. He had many burning questions and few answers. Legend has it that he sat meditating under the Bo tree for seven years until he reached enlightenment.

The etymological root of the word Buddha is, "Budh", which means to awaken. So, a Buddha is someone who through his own efforts develops a transformed view of the world. This transformation brings about a new mode of thinking, feeling, and being which has been referred to as reaching enlightenment.

There is an old saying that "If you meet the Buddha on the road, kill him!" This points to the importance of discovering your own Buddha-nature. You don't have to be Michael Jordan, Bill Gates, or a famous person in order to be happy, worthy, or fulfilled. It is only necessary to be the best person you can be.

There's a story about a woman named Barbara Foster. When she died, she was met at the gates of heaven by St. Peter. He didn't ask her, "How come you weren't like Mother Theresa or Oprah Winfrey?" But he did ask her, "How come you weren't the best Barbara Foster you could be?"

There is a saying that a short thing is the short body of Buddha and a long thing is the long body of Buddha. Let this sink into your bones and into your marrow. You are already fine the way you are, but you just don't believe it. Accept and love yourself even as you try to change and evolve, and, if you meet the Buddha on the road, kill him!

Babe Ruth

Years ago, I watched my daughter at bat in a little league game. It was the last inning and her team was losing by one run. The bases were loaded and there were two outs. The fans (crazed, irrational parents) for both teams were screaming. For a moment, it became surreal as I was blurring the boundary lines between her game and a scene from the movie, "The Natural", in which Robert Redford blasts a dramatic home run at a critical time. I snapped out of it and focused on my daughter. She looked like a statue at home plate. She stood rigidly and took three straight strikes without ever moving the bat. Game over.

Resisting the tendency to immediately lecture or show disappointment (she may have her own version of this story), I didn't talk to her about it until later that night. Being a Yankee fan, she had heard of Babe Ruth. I asked her to tell me about him. She said that he was "the homerun king".

I said to her, "That's right. He was the homerun king and that's how everyone remembers him. Nobody remembers him as the strikeout king even though he struck out more than anybody else." Her eyes lit up. I continued, "The reason he was able to hit so many homers is that he swung for the fences. He would go for it. He'd give it all he had. He'd give it his best shot."

It's okay to be nervous, but to become immobilized is not a solution. If you're going to strike out, take your best

101

swings in the process. Just give it your best shot. That's all anyone can really ask of you and all you can really ask of yourself.

Beans, Burgers, and Beliefs

I was raised in a meat eating family. Carnivores, every one of them. In fact, my five siblings and myself would frequently argue over who'd get the drumstick or the biggest steak. A meal was incomplete without meat. My wife came from a middle-eastern background and ground up raw lamb was a delicacy. Meat was the central part of our diets. Our families were skeptical and disapproving when we announced we'd become vegetarians. They were certain it was a fad, and a dangerous one at that. It's been 30 years since we've eaten meat, poultry, or fish.

There is a type of learning involving rote memory. We just get the same fact repeatedly until we remember it. This is usually how we learn multiplication or what's called the times table. We keep repeating 8 times 9 is 72 until we remember it. Rote learning.

This same kind of phenomenon happens when we are children and repeatedly exposed to the values of our parents and families. We learn what to value because we are told what is important and what isn't, what is right for us and what is wrong. As adults, we can reach our own conclusions, our own values. It may be that we decide much of what we learned is congruent with our values, but not the whole package, lock, stock, and barrel.

This is what my wife and I did when we decided to give up meat. We adopted not eating meat as our value and raised

103

our children from birth as vegetarians. We sent peanut butter and jelly sandwiches to the McDonald's birthday parties they attended. They ate beans, pasta, veggie versions of hot dogs and hamburgers, and dealt with the curiosity of their schoolmates. Now, as young adults with keen minds, they will have to decide upon their own values. They'll decide what's right for them, to be a carnivore or a vegetarian. It's important that they make the decision. They know our values. They have to discover theirs.

What have you learned that you do by rote, simply because you learned it? Think about the teachings you received dealing with health, sex, money, food, exercise, traveling, family, religion, friends, and so on. It's never too late to decide what is truly important to you and what isn't.

The Chicken Little Phenomenon

Many people live life in a chronic state of anxiety. They have difficulty relaxing. Always expecting that disaster is lurking around every corner, they are ever vigilant so as to recognize the earliest cues of the impending crisis. These people sometimes label themselves as born worriers and usually admit to coming from a family in which one or both parents were excellent at worrying. Chicken Little cried in dismay that "The sky is falling, the sky is falling!" after an apple (not a piece of the sky) hit her on the head. She became preoccupied with this notion to the extent that it interfered with her ability to engage in life in a cheerful, non-anxious manner.

Most of the worrying that we do serves no purpose. On rare occasions, worry can be helpful. For example, worrying a bit about a forthcoming test can help motivate you to prepare well for the exam. Or, worrying that you aren't sure how to get to your intended destination may lead to your seeking directions prior to your trip.

However, the majority of the worrying that people do is futile and useless, and doesn't influence what inevitably takes place. I know a man who has worried daily for the past twenty-three years that he might lose the job that he still has. I know a woman who worries frequently that her nineteen year-old daughter may eventually move to a different part of the country, although her daughter has absolutely no plans to do so.

Are there things you worry about much of the time that you have no control over? Most of the time you worry, it is the equivalent of walking over to the wall and beating your head against it. It is a useless, painful experience that leads to nothing constructive. Most of the things that you spend so much time worrying about never even happen. It's not necessary or helpful to worry in advance about anxiety provoking possibilities. If they do occur (and they may not) you'll have as much time as you need to worry about them!

In other words, most likely, "The sky is not falling. The sky is not falling!". But if it ever does, that's the time to start worrying about it. In the meantime, kick off your shoes, take a deep breath, and relax for a while.

What Do You Need?

Years ago I was intensely involved in Zen studies. I was looking forward to participating in my first sesshin. This would be three full days of meditation without a word being spoken. We would alternate sitting meditation (Zazen) with walking meditation (Kinhin), eat lots of beans and rice, clean toilets, and on the final day have a private meeting with the Zen Master (Dokusan). It was only at this dokusan that talking was allowed.

By the middle of the third day, I was a bit weary and my legs ached. I was eagerly anticipating my encounter with Soen Sa Nihm, a very celebrated Zen Master. As my time approached I found myself with a major flatulence problem and a growing need to relieve myself of three days worth of beans. I was trying to hold on, fearing that if I went to the bathroom I would miss my chance for having a dokusan.

I was soon tapped on the shoulder, indicating it was indeed my turn. For years I had thought about this moment. Finally, dokusan! Yet, all I could think about was my need to go to the bathroom. As I sat in a cross legged position on his special cushion, my leg pain immediately worsened and I passed gas (at least it was silent, thus in the spirit of the sesshin). I was consumed with my physiological needs and all I could think about was getting to a bathroom. If the Zen Master had any wisdom to impart, I was unable to receive it. I was thrilled when our interview ended and I headed directly to the bath-

107

room that I had laboriously cleaned the night before. Speaking of Nirvana.

Abraham Maslow was a psychologist who studied emotionally healthy individuals. He developed a hierarchy of needs that require satisfaction in order for a person to eventually feel self-actualized and fulfilled. When one level of needs is satisfied, the person is able to move on to the next level of needs.

At the bottom of the need hierarchy are the physiological needs of the person such as for hunger, thirst, and safety. If those needs are not satisfied, the person will not be able to go on to the next level of needs which are for belongingness and love. These are followed by needs for esteem, and needs for self-actualization. To be self-actualized is to be positive in outlook, accepting of self and others, creative, manifest a good sense of humor, have deep, satisfying interpersonal relationships, be independent, and deeply appreciate art and life.

The catch phrase that sums up Maslow's need hierarchy is "Bread before Bach". Unless your more primitive basic needs are met, it will be difficult for you to concentrate on and appreciate classical music. I would guess that if you are struggling somewhere on the hierarchy, it may be on the level of belongingness and love. It will be difficult for you to reach all your potentials and be happy and fulfilled unless you feel loved and have some meaningful sense of belongingness.

It could be to a family, a spiritual group, a community group, a support group, or any person or group of people that you can feel at home with and be yourself without fear of ridicule or rejection. If your needs are not met on the level of love and belongingness, make a concerted effort to involve yourself in arenas that could do it for you.

Oh yes, I remember the dokusan well. I guess, at least temporarily, I got stuck at the level of satisfying my basic needs. At that time, I had no interest in Bach, Zen Masters, or enlightenment. Sometimes, timing is everything.

Chickens, Bulls, and Elephants

I've worked with a lot of people who could be described as thin-skinned, overly sensitive, or easily hurt. It's not exactly that everything is a big deal to them, but many, if not most things are. If something unexpected occurs or if someone says something upsetting, they become unglued or fall to pieces. Part of what I do as a therapist is to help them develop a thicker skin and put the pieces together.

With the majority of situations, if someone gets bent out of shape about something, I'll help her reach the conclusion that it's not really a big deal. Much of what people get upset about is trivial. Other events happen that are less trivial. Although these happenings are to be taken more seriously, they can be dealt with by developing better coping techniques such as using rational self-talk, deep breathing, and positive action.

Occasionally something very serious happens. Although I recognize this will be difficult to deal with, I help the person realize that she can deal with it and that although it may seem it, it is not the end of the world.

Decades ago, a Gestalt psychologist named Fritz Perls got to the point in a crude but direct manner. To paraphrase his ideas, and to use his language, all things in life can be classified as being either "chicken-shit, bullshit, or elephant-shit". Perls believed that most people coming in for therapy need to learn to put more and more in the chicken-shit category and less and less in the other two compartments.

For example, someone may feel like 10% of their "prob-lems" are of the chicken variety, 40% bull, and 50% elephant. A good therapist or a good friend or even this book can help them to develop a less vulnerable skin and therefore perceive 80% of their "problems" as chicken-shit, 15% as bullshit, and 5% as elephant-shit.

When you're faced with a situation that you'd usually feel very upset by, ask yourself the question, "How important or traumatic is this really in the overall scheme of things?". And then see if you can feel okay about labeling it as chicken-shit (excuse my language!).

These terms are not meant to minimize your concerns but rather to get you to understand and believe that a lot of what gets you upset can be perceived differently and thought about differently. And this will lead you to conclude and feel that, "It's not a big deal".

Mr. Fix-It

My friends refer to me as "mechanically challenged". At the very least I would say that I'm not handy. I truly believe I have some undiagnosed, subtle perceptual problem, but no one is buying into that explanation. In grade school, I failed miserably at mechanical drawing. My woodshop projects always looked quite different from everyone else's. In high school, I did excellent in algebra but didn't have a clue in geometry. Standardized tests having problems dealing with spatial relationships baffled me. I would like to be handier but it's not an area I've made a great deal of progress in. It may be a "tragic flaw" in the classic sense of the term.

Taking advantage of a visit from Billy, an old college friend, I asked if he could look at an exercise bike that wasn't working well. He asked me to get him a hammer and went on to describe in detail to me what a hammer looked like. While he was fixing the bike, my wife walked in and quickly burst into a rendition of the old song, "It's so nice to have a man around the house". Okay, so my entire tool chest consists of two screwdrivers (one's a Phillips head) and a hammer. I feel secure enough not to base my self-image on whether I can put together a _____ (you can fill in the blank with almost any object you choose).

We all have some tragic flaw, be it physical, perceptual, character, or skill related. Try not to base your image of yourself on that flaw. Don't focus on the body part you don't like

111

about yourself or the thing you're not good at. Focus on the whole package and all the fine things about yourself. That's what I try to do. I'll be the first to admit that you shouldn't let me near any appliance you need dealt with, but call me if you need to talk about anything. And remember, go with the flow, not the flaw.

California, Here I Come

People sometimes seek what I have come to refer to as the "geographical cure". They may be dissatisfied with their lives, their jobs, or their relationships. They firmly believe moving to a new location will solve all their ills. This line of thinking is more common in young adults than it is in older adults who are more rooted in their areas.

Typically, three states come up over and over. Inevitably, those looking for the cure will mention either Colorado, Florida, or California. Maybe I don't hear New York because I live so close to it. Perhaps someone living out west may link the geographical cure to New York. I'm not certain. I've never heard Arkansas, Wisconsin, West Virginia, or just about any other state mentioned. I've gotten one or two North Carolinas.

I'm not a big believer in the geographical cure. That's because you take your psyche with you wherever you go. Wherever you go, you wind up in the here and now, and it's still you. You don't become a different person because you traveled a few thousand miles. Unless you're the tin man, scarecrow, or cowardly lion, but that's another story. If you want to feel better it's most likely more important to change the cognitive geography within your head than it is to change the state you live in.

A farmer living on the edge of town was milking one of her cows. A traveler on horseback arrives and asks her, "What's it like in this town that I'm coming into?".

She replies, "What was it like in the place you just left?"

He answers, "It was terrible. The people were selfish and unfriendly. Difficult to get along with. You know how it is."

The farmer responded, "I'm sorry to tell you that that's probably what you'll find in this town too."

"Yeah, that's what I thought," said the traveler as he rode toward the town.

Later that morning, another traveler arrives on horseback and asks the same farmer, "What's it like in this town I'm coming into?"

She asks, "What was it like in the place you just left?"

He answers, "The people were real nice. Friendly. I got along with just about everyone."

The farmer responded, "That's most likely what you'll find in this town too."

"That's what I thought," said the traveler as he rode toward the town.

Take a Deep Breath (or Fifty)

We all know of the folk wisdom advising us to "take a deep breath" to help us deal with an issue, regain our composure, or feel better in general. It is good advice. It can help settle us physiologically or psychologically speaking. Do it right now. Take a long slow deep breath that starts from below your belly button and gently exhale it. I wouldn't be surprised if you feel a pinch better than you did twenty seconds ago.

Now, find a quiet spot with some privacy and instead of simply taking a deep breath, take fifty deep breaths. If one deep breath has the capacity to be beneficial, imagine what fifty can do. Sit up straight in a chair, close your eyes, and breathe abdominally. Your belly should expand rather than your chest. Breathe deeply (not noisily or dramatically) through your nose, gently inhaling a thin narrow stream of air until your belly fills. Then, gently exhale the air through your nose.

It's as if a balloon in your belly slowly fills with air and is then very slowly compressed to bring the air back up and out your nose. Every time you inhale, say the number of the breath silently to yourself and repeat the same number on the exhalation. Start with number one and go to fifty. Depending on your rate of breathing, this may take you ten to twenty minutes. If fifty seems too much, start with ten and work your way up adding five breaths each week.

115

Focus all your awareness on counting your breaths. Whatever else comes into your mind, simply let go of it and return your awareness fully to your breathing. Whatever comes into your mind is okay. Just always let go of it and bring all your consciousness back to your breathing.

The word "breath" derives from the Latin "spiritus" which conveys air, life, soul, and spirit. Breathing exercises have been an important part of spiritual practices and more recently, medical practices.

You've probably heard the expression "take five". Well, when it comes to taking deep breaths, take five, ten,...or even, "take fifty".

<u>Us and Them</u>

Do you have any preconceived ideas about people of different races or religions? How about fat people? What about those who are very short, or bald, or those who pierce their noses? Think carefully before answering. Do you cling to any stereotyped notions with respect to people's nationalities? Examine your prejudices. Sometimes you have them because that is what you were taught. It could be a bit scary to openly deal with people who seem strange, so you find ways of categorizing them, making sense of them so as to minimize your anxiety and know what to expect.

In essence, you've divided the world into us and them. "Us" comprises you and everyone who shares certain important characteristics and ideology with you. "Them" are those who are different. They may look different, act different, or express different viewpoints.

No matter what a person looks like, dresses like, or sounds like, she still has a need to be loved and respected, to love, and to have a sense of belongingness. I think the bottom line is that we are more alike than different.

The Zen Master Seung Sahn makes the point that in a cookie factory, cookies come in all different forms. Some are large and others small. They may be shaped like stars, people, animals, or buses, but they are all made from the same dough. It's all the same substance although the cookies appear quite different. And so it is with you and me and people who appear so different. We're all made from the same dough.

It Will Never Be This Day Again

It was a beautiful spring day with a deep blue sky and a cool breeze. My 80 year-old mother-in-law, Alma, was softly singing to herself in the backyard as she sorted through clothespins to hang her laundry on the line. To her, it was the perfect day for laundry. To me, it was the perfect day for tennis. Tennis, laundry, it really didn't matter because we were both seizing the day. Carpe Diem. This day will never come again. There will never be another May 12, 2003. Never.

I try to get better and better at seizing more and more days. It's easier to seize the sunny summer days when I'm on vacation than it is to seize the rainy November days when I'm working, but I'm getting much better at narrowing the gap. Independent of weather, where I'm at, who I'm with, or whether I'm at work or play, I try to do my best to do away with all my judgmental distinctions and closed minded preferences, seize the moment and seize the day. Try not to let your preconceived notions of what is enjoyable and not enjoyable taint the quality of your day, and Carpe Diem.

There is the story of a man who was traveling across a field when a tiger began to chase him. He came to the edge of a cliff where he took hold of a wild vine and swung himself over the edge. The tiger growled at him from above. Trembling, he looked down, where far below another tiger was waiting to eat him. Only the vine sustained him. Two mice,

119

one white and one black, little by little, started to gnaw away the vine. The man saw a luscious strawberry near him. Grasping the vine with one hand, he plucked the strawberry with the other. How sweet it tasted!

Do You Have Time?

I have an important question to ask you and I'm not going to beat around the bush. I'm simply going to ask you flat out. Do you really have time for regrets, bad moods, whining, moaning, groaning, and complaining? I don't mean to lack compassion or trivialize your concerns, but I want to get right to the point, right to the heart of the matter. The obituaries in today's paper stated that the ages of those who died were 63, 51, 19, 34, 86, 73, 56, 91, 11, 29, and 49.

Is it getting clearer what I'm talking about? Are you close to the age of anyone in those obituaries? What are you doing with your precious time?

The German artist Kathe Kollwitz draws death lurking waiting to tap you on the shoulder at any time. This realization is not meant to depress you but rather to add vitality to your life. Don't approach life as if you're certain you have plenty of time and will die of old age. When things are not going particularly well for you, don't get caught in a downward spiral of negative thinking. The antidote for negative thinking is positive action. Whether you have 6 months or 60 years left is uncertain. Use your time well.

Once again let me remind you, this is not a dress rehearsal. So think about the question and let it sink into your bones and into your marrow. Do you really have time for regrets, bad moods, whining, moaning, groaning, and complaining?

121

Don't Expect Things to Be Perfect

The word for a perfect place is Utopia. The literal Greek translation of Utopia is U/No and Topia/Place. In other words, the perfect place is no place. You can count on traffic jams, people being late, and an occasional cold or flu. When dealing with people, inevitably the "check is in the mail" and the "computer system is down". The weather won't necessarily cooperate with your plans, and now and again, you can be sure of a poor night's sleep. We do not always feel terrific. Witness the supermarket aisle containing Anacin, Excedrin, Tylenol, Tums, Rolaids, and hundreds of other formulas intended for relief of pain or discomfort.

If the only way for you to be happy is for the world to unfold according to your expectations of how things should be, you're in trouble. Things will most likely never be exactly as you would like them to be. Instead of getting bent out of shape over the discrepancy between your expectations and reality, cultivate the traits of tolerance and acceptance.

My friend Toni told me a story I'd like to share with you. She's a social worker for a large bureaucratic county welfare agency. Life there is filled with red tape, forms in triplicate, and a high volume of people. One day, a frazzled woman arrived at closing time eager to find out when her newly assigned caseworker would be calling her for an appointment. Almost everyone had left for the day. To appease the woman, Toni agreed to at least check the files to see which worker had been assigned to this new case and then write a note for the worker to call the woman.

After tracking down the information, Toni returned smiling and said to the woman, "Just to show you the perfection of the universe, I checked on it and as it turns out, I am your caseworker." When Toni told me this story, I wondered how she would have responded if it turned out that it was Jack Myers and not Toni who was the woman's caseworker. Would she have said to the woman, "Just to show you the perfection of the universe, I checked on it and as it turns out, I am not your caseworker."

Ask yourself whether your day really is ruined simply because something occurred that wasn't according to the script that you had in mind. You can't control what people say or don't say, or what they do or don't do. But you can control how you respond to those situations.

You are sharing your neighborhood, community, state, country, and world with lots of other people. That is part of the bargain. Hopefully, most of the time they will be friendly, helpful, and compassionate. But you can count on times when they will be rude, annoying, scary, or hostile.

If you insist upon focusing on the gap between how you wish things unfolded and how they actually unfolded, you will be creating anxiety, sadness, frustration, or other emotions that contribute to your not feeling well and happy. Remember, this is not Utopia. The "perfect place" is "no place". Other people and their quirks, idiosyncrasies, and character traits come along with the territory.

"In that direction," the Cat said, waving its right paw round, "lives a Hatter: and in that direction," waving the other paw, "lives a March Hare. Visit either you like: they're both mad."

123

"But I don't want to go among mad people," Alice remarked.

"Oh, you can't help that," said the Cat.

(*Alice In Wonderland*)

The Wise Man

It was a beautiful afternoon in late May when a father took his four year old son for a stroll in the park. Just about everything was in bloom and the day was vivid Technicolor.

The little boy asked his father, "Daddy, why is the sky blue?"

His father answered, "That's a good question, but I'm really not sure, son."

Later, the boy queried, "Dad, why is the grass green?"

The father replied, "Gee, I really don't know."

A few minutes thereafter, the little boy once again was curious. "Daddy, why do ducks quack?"

His father said, "I'm uncertain."

His son responded, "Daddy, do you mind me asking so many questions?"

To which his father answered, "Of course not son, how else are you going to learn?"

Sometimes, obtaining factual information is less important than the experience occurring in the attempt to get that information. What matters here is not whether the father knew the answers. Other issues transcend that. We have the bonding of a father and son as they walk side by side through a park. They experience nature and all its wonder. They take in the sights and sounds of a gorgeous spring day. The father does not get angry with his son for asking so many questions and he does not get down on himself for not knowing the answers. He remains loving and interested. Despite his being unable to answer the "simple" questions, the father is a wise man.

What Do You Think?

Once upon a time a peasant found an eagle's egg and put it in the nest of a backyard hen along with the hen's eggs. The eaglet hatched and was raised with the chicks that hatched at the same time. He and the backyard chickens scratched the earth for worms, clucked and cackled, thrashed their wings and flew a few feet into the air. The eagle grew old.

One day he saw a magnificent bird gliding across the deep blue sky. It was graceful and strong. The old eagle was in awe and asked, "Who's that?". His neighbor replied, "That's the eagle, king of the birds. He belongs to the sky. We chickens belong to the earth." So the eagle lived and died a chicken, for that's what he thought he was.

What do you think you are? Do you impose limits on yourself without realizing it? There's a saying that if you think you can, you can, and if you think you can't, you can't. Another way of putting it is, if you think you can or think you can't, you're right.

My children and my wife are good skiers. I'm not. We went to the top of a mountain in Vermont. They took a black diamond (expert) trail called "Ripcord" while I opted for a blue square (intermediate) named "Skyline". We agreed to meet an hour later. I skied the trail a couple of times and made it down okay despite having a fairly rough time doing so.

Later, I took them all to ski the trail with me. It turned out that I had misread the signs and, without realizing it, had

127

skied "Freefall", one of the harder black diamonds. If I had read the signs correctly, I never would have attempted to ski "Freefall" because I wouldn't have thought I'd be able to do it. That's how I skied my first black diamond.

A Little Bit Better

It's happened to me. I'm almost certain it's happened to you. We can be pretty certain it will happen again. I'm talking about a crisis. It's a word that has to be taken seriously. It is derived from the Greek krisis which indicates a decision and a turning point.

When my daughter was 7 years old she developed cerebella ataxia from an infection that went to her brain. She lost all coordination. She was unable to sit up without projectile vomiting. She was unable to use her limbs or her body. She couldn't walk or talk. Needless to say, this was an extremely frightening time for all of us. After a week in the hospital, the infectious diseases specialist told us that she would probably recover all her functions. Although it was difficult to do, I decided to believe him.

During her hospital stay and throughout her rehabilitation, I spent a great deal of time with Jenna. Our motto was, "A little bit better every day. A little bit better in every way." It was joyous when she began to be able to sit up. We celebrated when she took her first step, and later when she could put a few words together for the first time. Jenna's illness and eventual recovery gave me the chance to truly be with her in a time of need and to once again realize how much we all take for granted. Although she's now 22 years old, I think about her illness every day and give thanks for her recovery.

The Chinese calligraphy for the word crisis is made up of two characters, one being the character for danger and the other one being the character for opportunity. Think about that. A crisis, by virtue of definition, will be challenging and perhaps risky or scary. But it can also provide you with an opportunity to grow stronger or be more compassionate or be important in the life of another person. In a difficult time it is important to believe that you can reach deep within yourself and harness those resources necessary to cope with and ultimately get beyond the crisis. And remember, "A little bit better everyday, a little bit better in every way."

Shocking News

As little children, we are bombarded with ongoing dictates such as, "Respect your elders", "Listen to your teachers", and "Do what you are told". There's nothing wrong with respecting authority figures. That is, unless they don't deserve our respect. Respecting authority is not the same as having blind obedience to authority.

A famous social psychology experiment produced some very disturbing results. The subject being tested was told to deliver a series of electric shocks to a person sitting near him but out of his sight. That out of sight person was not really being shocked but was pretending to be, and would scream louder and louder as the shocks became more powerful.

The person being tested could actually see on a gauge the intensity of the shock and when it got into a range labeled "dangerous". The authority figure (the professor in the white coat) would tell the person to keep increasing the power of the shocks. Despite the screams of the person purportedly being shocked and despite the meter reading "dangerous", a high percentage of people being tested continued to deliver the shocks. Such is the phenomenon of obedience to authority.

Let me suggest that your own experience is the highest authority. Trust yourself. If it doesn't feel right to you, it's probably not the right thing to do. We have been abused or at least mislead and mistreated by clergy, CEO's, bosses, civil servants, and presidents. You cannot assume that a powerful

131

person is fair or moral or ethical. Some rules, policies, and procedures may continue to exist even though they are no longer useful or in anyone's best interest.

When the spiritual teacher and his disciples began their evening meditation, the cat who lived in the monastery made such noise that it distracted them. So the teacher ordered that the cat be tied up each evening. Years later, when the teacher died, the cat continued to be tied up during the nighttime meditation session. And when the cat eventually died, another cat was brought to the monastery and tied up. Centuries later, learned descendants of the spiritual teacher wrote scholarly treatises about the religious significance of tying up a cat each night during meditation practice.

Understand How Powerful Your Thoughts Can Be

Suppose you were invited to a house party where you were going to meet all new people. A few days prior to the party, you passed a store that had an unusual outfit in the window. It was not like any other outfit you owned and it indeed would be a markedly different style of dress than what you were used to. On impulse, you buy the outfit, believing you may be on the brink of impressing a group of new people at the upcoming party.

Scenario #1: You walk into the living room of the party and five or six people turn and look at you. You quickly feel a significant amount of anxiety. Your heart is beating rapidly and you begin to sweat. You feel like leaving the party as quickly as possible. What has happened is something like this. You thought to yourself, "Oh my God, look at them staring at me. Why did I buy this ridiculous looking outfit? I must look like an idiot!"

Scenario #2: It's the same party and you're wearing the same outfit. You walk into the living room and the same five or six people turn and look at you. You feel great, confident, and eager to meet new people. You have probably told yourself something to the effect of, "Wow, I'm really turning heads tonight. I'm glad I bought this outfit".

Scenario #3: Same party. Same outfit. Same heads turn and look at you. You neither feel like running out of the room or like you're on top of the world. You feel O.K. Most likely you told yourself something such as, "It's natural for people to turn and look when someone new enters the party. It doesn't mean a great deal one way or the other".

The only thing different in these three scenarios is what you have told yourself about the heads turning to look at you. Everything else is exactly the same. Yet, you have three totally different feelings and experiences based solely upon what you have told yourself about the situation.

Think about it. No one in any of the three scenarios did or said anything to contribute to how you felt in those situations. That is, no one but you. This is a simple and clear example of how, in many instances, you create your feelings. Letting this sink in is a way of feeling less out of control and more empowered.

<u>Getting Things In Focus</u>

How do you spend your time? I'm talking about your mental time. What goes on in your head all day long? What do you choose to focus on? We have endless choices all day as to whether we want to attend to this, that, or the other thing.

There was a spinster who lived by herself in an old house at the edge of a small rural town. One day she looked out her window and saw two young boys skinny-dipping in the river. She phoned the sheriff. He arrived and told the boys to get out of there. They moved along.

About a half hour later, the woman looked out her window and spotted the same boys skinny -dipping again. This time they were about a hundred and fifty yards down the river. Once again she called the sheriff who promptly came and got rid of the youngsters. Forty-five minutes later, the sheriff got a third call from the old woman. She again complained that the same boys were skinny -dipping.

The sheriff was very surprised and asked her if she was sure it was the same boys. She said, "Oh, they're not very close, but I'm almost certain it's them. They're a bit difficult to see, but if I stand on a chair and look out the small attic window, I can see them through my binoculars."

What are you going out of your way to focus on? There may be other ways for you to spend your mental time. It may be in your best interest to focus on other things.

One day a man of the people said to Zen Master Ikkyu, "Master, would you please write for me some maxims of the highest wisdom."

Ikkyu immediately took his brush and wrote the word "Attention".

"Is that all?" asked the man. "Would you not add something more?"

Ikkyu then wrote twice running: "Attention. Attention."

"Well," remarked the man rather irritably. "I really don't see much depth in what you have just written."

Then Ikkyu wrote the same word three times running: "Attention. Attention. Attention."

Half angered, the man demanded, "What does that word 'Attention' mean anyway?"

Ikkyu answered gently, "Attention means attention."

Neurosis is a term indicating an existence characterized by anxiety and unhappiness. The distinguished psychologist Alfred Adler once said that neurosis is largely a matter of attention.

Isness

Buddha said life is frustration. There is suffering. Nothing lasts. Meetings end in separation. Buildings eventually destruct. All forms ruin sooner or later. Much of the time it seems you don't get what you want and get what you don't want.

He said that the cause of frustration is wanting things to be different than they are at any given time. Clinging to your notions that things should be perfect or at least different then they are leads to frustration.

Buddha believed the solution was an acceptance of "isness". <u>When any given moment unfolds, it can only be just the way it is at that particular moment.</u> That's isness. All you ever do is decide how to deal with isness. Legend has it that the Sun-faced Buddha lives 1800 years while the Moon-faced Buddha lives only one night. While we're working to create change, things are just as they are. According to Lao Tsu:

> Sometime breathing is hard,
> Sometimes easy.
> Sometimes there is strength and
> Sometimes there is weakness.
> The universe is perfect
> You cannot improve it.

This is not a philosophy of fate or determinism. Even though things are perfect in the strange way that they can only be as they are (the truth) at any moment, we still do everything we can do to improve our quality of life, have peace in the world, and so on. The paradox is that things are perfect (not in a Utopian way but in the sense that any moment cannot be different than it is when it unfolds), and yet we need to continue to work on ourselves to get things to be better. There is isness, but there is still freedom of choice. They are neither incompatible nor mutually exclusive.

Ram Dass, in 'The Only Dance There Is', tells of a guru and about 200 spiritual seekers who were meditating silently in a large New York City loft that was located near a firehouse. Every once in awhile the fire engines would be called out and the loud sounds of the sirens would fill the room. You could see the pained expressions of the participants. It was as if, "Those damned fire engines ruined our spiritual gathering!". But, the guru thought, "There is the fire engine and that's the way it is."

There is no other reality for that here and now moment. Once it occurs, it can only be exactly as it is at that moment. So, Buddha says stop clinging to the notion of how things should be different than they are, accept isness, and invest yourself fully in getting things to be better for you (although they're already perfect).

Taking Out the Garbage

Twice a week or so I take out the garbage. Usually, it's in plastic bags or sometimes paper bags that I've brought home from the supermarket. I put them in garbage cans and secure the lids with bungee straps to keep the raccoons and the deer from making a mess. This is a ritual I've engaged in for years.

I'm not sure how Webster defines garbage, but I consider it things that are no longer useful. Scraps, remnants, broken items, rotting objects in various stages of decomposition and the like. Things that have worn out, that no longer serve any useful purpose, and which take up space and demand our attention. Once, these items may have played some role of significance in my life, but now they are garbage and need to be gotten rid of. It's time.

It strikes me that all of us accumulate what could be termed emotional garbage. Residue from all sorts of past experiences and relationships. Traumas, rejections, abusive interactions, critical teachers or parents, betrayals, embarrassing encounters, feelings of shame or guilt or inadequacy, and other childhood and adolescent fears and feelings that still haunt or taunt us. I think that at least twice a week, it's a good idea to take out the emotional garbage.

For example, every Monday and Thursday, vividly imagine yourself filling a garbage bag with all your thoughts, experiences, and feelings that are no longer useful to have in your mind/body. Get rid of everything that doesn't work for

139

you, that weighs you down, and that is rotting within you. Put it all in the bag and take it out and dump it in the garbage can. Secure the lid on the can. You may not have given it a lot of thought before this, but taking out the garbage is a very important thing to do.

For Lou Gehrig, Catfish Hunter, and Countless Others

Imagine you have a terminal disease that slowly but surely effects your muscles and your nervous system. You will deteriorate everyday. You will lose control of your body and be unable to carry out even simple daily tasks of living. Imagine this vividly. More vividly. Even more vividly. How do you feel? Is there terror, dread, depression? Picture yourself entrenched in the position I've described above. See yourself unable to walk, unable to work, socialize, or participate in life as you have lived it until now.

You might bargain with God. Something to the effect of, "Dear God, if I recover, I'll be a different person. I'll be a better person, a more loving and compassionate person. I'll be a better wife, mother, sister, daughter. I'll give more of myself to those in need. Please, dear God, please!"

Now, imagine that your prayers have been answered. You discover that indeed you will recover and have normal working muscles and a normal nervous system. You can walk, hop, skip, jump, and run. You can participate fully in life. Now what? Do you make the changes that you promised to make? Are you eternally grateful and see each day as a gift? Or, do you quickly fall into your old habits and routines?

Your life can change in an instant. Don't take anything for granted. You have been given another day, another chance. You can be alive, awake, and thankful, and make good on your

141

promise to be different. Or, you can be semi-unconscious, going through life on automatic pilot and bemoaning your plight in life, with each day being somewhat of an instant replay of the previous day. You do not have that debilitating, terminal disease. What are you going to do about it?

<u>Swept Away</u>

Recently, a professional athlete turned down a contract offer of over 20 million dollars a year. It wasn't enough money. And this was for playing baseball. He wanted to make over $150,000 each time he played a game. This man is a hero in our society.

When a family member was recuperating in a local hospital, I stopped by to see her early each morning so as to lend a hand with breakfast. Each day, the same hospital employee would come in to sweep the room, and each day we spoke to each other a bit more. He gave the room a very thorough sweeping and seemed to enjoy what he was doing. We chatted about the Mets and Yankees and baseball in general. He was a true fan.

Intelligence wise, he may have been considered a little on the slow side, but he was smart enough to think it astonishing (my word to match the expression on his face) that a baseball player would turn down an offer of over 20 million dollars a year. We joked about it. I enjoyed our brief daily visits. He always offered a hearty good morning greeting as well as some encouraging words. And he pushed his broom with a sense of purpose and obviously took pride in his efforts.

As the weeks went by, I learned he was in his late fifties and that he worked at that same hospital in that same capacity for his entire adult life. He pushed a broom through those

143

hospital corridors for 41 consecutive years. Forty-one years of cleaning up after everyone and doing so with pride and a cheerful disposition.

Oh, and speaking of astonishment (as I was doing a few minutes ago), it turned out that he had not missed one day of work in those 41 years. Not one! I thought to myself that he works everyday for four years to make the same amount of money that baseball player makes for playing one game. I really don't know that baseball player personally, and I don't hold his extraordinary talent against him. But, if a hero is someone you look up to, respect, admire his accomplishments, and feel privileged to meet or be with, I'll take the guy who sweeps the hospital.

Start a New Tradition

After hearing the same complaint from a number of people, I came up with an idea and offered it to them. Their complaint was that they didn't get to spend time with certain valued friends or relatives on Thanksgiving. In some cases it was due to splitting holidays, i.e., one Thanksgiving with his family and the next with her family. In other instances, the friends or loved ones were invited elsewhere. My idea was to have another Thanksgiving either the weekend before or after the actual Thanksgiving. You could invite anyone you wanted without putting them in conflict as to where they were going to spend Thanksgiving. You could do all friends or all relatives, or any combination you desired.

At least five people that I know of took me up on this suggestion. They later told me it had worked out well and they hoped it would be a new tradition for them. There's something very comforting about traditions if they are meaningful for you. Some traditions may not be conducive to your mental health if they are associated with family tensions or disappointments. I like the idea of adhering to time tested traditions that you look forward to, but also of creating new traditions that work well for you and your family or friends.

For ten straight years, my wife, myself, and our children have spent their winter break each February going skiing at the same ski area in Vermont. This became a tradition that we all looked forward to each year. Other traditions that we created include a group hug each night following the lighting of the Chanukah candles, a pancake breakfast after opening the gifts on Christmas (we celebrate just about everything), and taking pictures each year on the first day of school.

These are traditions that we came up with. In other words, these things were not done in our families of origin. We look forward to them each year. And, we are not about to rest on our laurels. We look forward to establishing additional traditions as the years go by. How about you bringing your creativity and passion to a new tradition? George Bernard Shaw said:

> Life is no brief candle to me. It is sort of a splendid torch which I have got hold of for a moment, and I want to make it burn as brightly as possible before handing it on to the future generations.

It Came Down to This

He was one helluva decent guy. Most of the time he was gentle and patient. On those rare occasions when he lost his temper, phew!! He worked hard but valued his leisure time. Disciplined beyond belief, but with many passions. He ran over 20 marathons, but his favorite was the 100th anniversary of the Boston Marathon in which he walked the whole way because of an injury that prevented him from running. He touched every one of the thousands of outstretched hands of the children lining the marathon route. He ran for charity.

As a psychologist and nutritionist, he helped many people and tried to help those who unfortunately didn't benefit from their meetings with him. He had terrific friends and was lucky enough to be "best man" for 3 of them. All in all, he was a lucky guy. Eclectic in his tastes, he was somehow never able to develop a fondness for either rap or country music. Had a bunch of faults but accepted them all. Wrote haiku poetry, and not a bad amateur photographer.

But above all he loved and cared for his family. Learned that from his own parents. One of 6 kids, learned early about the importance of family. Loved his wife Nan and prayed each day to be a better husband and father. His boy and girl twins, Dave and Jen meant everything to him and he gave them all he could in many different ways. He enjoyed life and considered himself blessed.

You just read my obituary. What would you like your obituary to say? How would you like to be remembered? I'd like you to write your obituary. Write your eulogy and your epitaph. Read carefully what you've written. If you do not care for your obituary, remember this – IT IS NOT TOO LATE TO DO SOMETHING ABOUT IT. You still have the time to make changes, now, before it is too late. Time is of the essence. Get started. Do something about it now so that the next time you write your obituary, you'll have a smile on your face.

Maya

"Maya", a Buddhist term, refers to the world as an illusion. This does not literally mean that the physical universe does not exist. Maya refers to experiencing the world in its full relativity, and realizing that the reality of our world is dependent upon our interpretations, our language, logic, and our arbitrary categorizations. In other words, to a very large degree, you create your own world. How you define events, people, and yourself influences how you experience life.

If you define something as a problem, it will immediately become problematic and the cause of much concern. That yellow dandelion, is it a weed or a flower? If it is defined as a weed it is a problem. It must be gotten rid of – weed killer, digging, plucking, and the like. If it is defined as a flower, you can enjoy it in all its splendor.

The word Maya comes from the Sanskrit root "Matr" which means to measure. The WORLD instead of being perceived in its ONENESS is measured and divided into pieces or things. So, it becomes us and them, the good guys and the bad guys, this and that and the other. Egocentricity, harsh judgment, territoriality, and policies of exclusion all stem from Maya.

Four blind men went to the zoo and visited the elephant. One of them touched the elephant's side and said, "The elephant is like a wall." The next blind man touched its trunk

149

and said, "The elephant is like a snake." The third blind man touched its leg and said, "The elephant is like a column." The last blind man touched its tail and said, "The elephant is like a broom."

Each blind man believed that his opinion was the right one. Each only understood the part he had touched. Each was stuck in his own vantage point. None of them understood the whole elephant.

Take It Off the Drawing Board

The saying has been around for along time. It's sometimes attributed to Lao Tsu. You may have gotten it in a fortune cookie.

The journey of a thousand miles begins with one step.

There is more wisdom in this than you might imagine. Making that initial move is crucial if your journey is to begin. Without it, you merely have ideas, plans, hopes, and goals, but haven't taken a step toward actualizing them.

If you have an elevator phobia, your first step might be to walk into a building that has an elevator. This is the way to begin. It is unrealistic to believe you should start by riding to the thirtieth floor. That would be like taking the thousand-mile journey in one gigantic anxiety provoking leap. Your second step might be to walk into the elevator when the door opens and quickly walk out again. Your third step might be to eventually ride one floor. Your tenth step might be to ride the elevator to the top floor.

This sequence may play out over a period of days, weeks, or months. You reach your destination through a series of successive approximations, behaviors which systematically lead you closer and closer to your goal.

If your goal is to learn golf and be able to play a decent eighteen holes, your first step might be to consult a pro for a lesson and get some advice. Step two may be to obtain clubs. Step three could be practicing at a driving range. Step four may be more lessons. Step five could be playing a round of golf.

If you are developing a new skill, there is no substitute for practice. Be patient. It might feel awkward for awhile. The same is true of learning mental or psychological skills. As you practice handling your anger, communicating differently, or talking to yourself more rationally, it will probably feel quite unnatural. Keep practicing. Eventually, it will feel less awkward and more second nature to you.

Each of us has things on the drawing board, some of which have been there for years. Prioritize. Pick something that's your equivalent to the journey of 1000 miles and by all means take that vital first step.

The Placebo Effect

In case you still had any doubts about how important your thoughts, attitude, and beliefs are in influencing both your psychological and physiological well-being, I have three words for you: the placebo effect.

A recent study published in the New England Journal of Medicine found that sham surgery was just as beneficial as regular arthroscopic knee surgery for arthritis. It wasn't that the real surgery was ineffective, but rather that the sham surgery was also effective. Think about this. People who were having pain and difficulty walking because of arthritic knees had what they thought was real arthroscopic surgery to repair the area. Although they didn't actually get the real surgery, they walked better, faster, and had less knee pain for the next two years. Hmmmmm.

Another recent study dealt with depressed people given either major antidepressant medication or placebo pills. The placebo group did as well as the group actually taking the genuine antidepressants. Science Magazine recently reported that Swedish and Finnish researchers had shown that placebos activate the same brain circuits as painkilling drugs. This could suggest that the placebo response is actually part of all painkilling treatments.

In May, 2002, researchers analyzed 96 studies that showed that people who receive sugar pills responded just as well to the "treatment" as those who took real medicines. This

153

research suggests a genuine placebo effect, and that people's minds and bodies react to placebos similarly to as if they received real medicines and treatments.

If you expect to get better from a treatment you believe in, chances are that you will. If you expect not to get better, chances are that is exactly what will happen. Your beliefs will affect your level of perceived pain, your brain circuitry, your immune system, your biochemistry, your healing, and your psychological well-being.

A doctor's office was filled with patients suffering from various seasonal allergies. When a delivery person came into the waiting room carrying several large floral arrangements, most of the patients began sneezing or wheezing. They didn't know that the arrangements were done with artificial flowers.

September 11th

September 11th, 2001 was a very sad day for the U.S. and also for US (that's us with a capital U and a capital S). US being the individuals (you and me) that make up our country. It is an understatement that aside from our collective pain, insecurity consumed us. Think about how we responded. We reached out to get connected. We called loved ones. We gathered in small groups. We helped at ground zero. We gave more money to relief efforts than ever before. The attitude was not "I gave at the office".

On September 11th, we reached out for each other and we reached inside our hearts. I'm not sure what the experience was like outside of the New York Metropolitan area, but within it, it was obvious that people were nicer and were banding together in a time of unprecedented insecurity in our nation. That infamous day brought out potentials that usually lie dormant in us. We cared more about each other. We briefly transcended categorizing others according to race, religion, occupation, status, looks, height, weight, or intelligence level. We were all briefly connected and shared the same plight.

Almost two years later, I have mixed feelings as things slowly return to "normal". It is nice to feel less threatened and have more of a feeling of security. But, can't we do that and hold onto each other at the same time? I believe that Jung once said something to the effect that life is like a terminal illness since it is the condition of which the prognosis is death.

This is our predicament. Make that OUR predicament. Not just on September 11th or in times of obvious danger, but everyday.

We need to let it sink in that WE are all carrying a burden, that we are all carrying a heavy load as we grapple with the day-to-day demands of living while recognizing our finiteness. We need to care for each other not because a September 11th like event occurred, but because WE can help each other lighten OUR loads. We all have secret burdens but also shared ones and need to be there for each other in small and large ways on a day-to-day basis. If we can do it in times of crisis, we can do it other times as well.

Years ago at a workshop, Ram Dass (American guru and former Harvard Professor Richard Alpert) said,

> In India, when we meet or part, we often say "Namaste", which means I honor the place in you where the entire universe resides. I honor the place in you of love, of light, of truth, of peace. I honor the place within you where if you are in that place in you and I am in that place in me, there is only one of us.

Going the Distance

It was the 2001 edition of the Boston Marathon. Katie Lynch, like most first-time marathoners, felt nervous. She was hoping to successfully negotiate all 26.2 feet of her race. That's right, not 26.2 miles. 26.2 feet. Lynch, who is afflicted with serious circulatory problems and back pain, gets around mostly with a walker or a wheelchair. In infancy, she was wrongly diagnosed with retardation and doctors predicted she would die young. She proved them wrong on both accounts.

The 27 year-old Lynch was definitely not retarded. She graduated from college summa cum laude and now works at Boston Children's Hospital and does motivational speaking on the side. Did I mention that Ms. Lynch is 28 inches tall and weighs 35 pounds? She was born with an unidentified type of dwarfism.

I want you to imagine yourself being 28 inches tall. Picture yourself in a variety of situations. Can you see yourself in a shopping mall, on the beach, in school, or at work? What does it feel like? Just imagine what Katie Lynch goes through on a daily basis.

Wearing the race number 2001, a baseball cap, and purple sneakers, Katie lined up at the starting line of the Boston Marathon. She had trained long and hard for this day. As she crossed the finish line of her 26.2 feet marathon, she shed tears of joy and the enthusiastic crowd cheered wildly. She said, "It was the most amazing thing," and "I don't think it could have

been more satisfying." Ms. Lynch seems to be living by a cre-
do we could all adopt. That is, do what you can with what
you have as long you can.

What is the true measure of a person? Technically speaking, Katie Lynch is a dwarf. But I think everyone would agree
she has the heart of a giant and immeasurable courage.

The Second Time Around

Nadine Stair, an 85 year-old woman from Kentucky wrote: "If I had my life to live over, I'd dare to make more mistakes next time. I'd relax, I'd limber up. I would be sillier than I've been this trip. I would take fewer things seriously, take more chances, take more trips. I'd climb more mountains and swim more rivers. I would eat more ice cream and less beans. I would perhaps have more actual troubles, but I'd have fewer imaginary ones.

You see, I'm one of those people who lived seriously, sanely, hour after hour, day after day. Oh, I've had my moments, and if I had it to do over again, I'd have more of them. I've been one of those persons who never goes anywhere without a thermometer, a hot water bottle, a raincoat, and a parachute. If I had to do it again, I would travel lighter than this trip. If I had my life to live over, I would start going barefoot earlier in the spring, and stay that way later in the fall. I would go to more dances, I would ride more merry-go-rounds. I would pick more daisies."

You may not have your whole life to live over, but you can start now to author it so that you'll have fewer regrets.

I began working with Mel when he was 79 years old and his wife of over fifty years passed away. I was there to help him deal with his sadness and his emptiness. He met Ann when she was 70. Her husband and the father of her five children had abruptly left twenty years ago. She did not have

159

an intimate relationship with a man since then. Trust was an issue.

Fast-forward two years. Mel and Ann see each other daily. They walk in the park regularly and play doubles tennis three times a week. They seek out romantic spots for dinner as well as new jazz combos to listen to. They are thrilled with their sexual relationship and care deeply about each other. They are authoring the latter chapters of their life in a way that has surprised them. They are taking Nadine Stair's advice. Mel dances as if no one is watching. Ann loves like she's never been hurt.

It's Not As Bad As You Think

There once was a monastery that was very strict. Following a vow of silence, no one was allowed to speak at all. But there was one exception to this rule. Every ten years, the monks were permitted to speak just two words. After spending his first ten years at the monastery, one monk went to see the head monk. "It has been ten years," said the head monk. "What are the two words you would like to speak?"

"Bed...hard..." said the monk.

"I see," replied the head monk.

Ten years later, the monk returned to the head monk's office. "It has been ten more years," said the head monk. "What are the two words you would like to speak?"

"Food stinks," said the monk.

"I see," replied the head monk.

Yet another ten years passed and the monk once again met with the head monk who asked, "What are the two words you would like to say?"

"Too cold," said the monk.

"Hmmmm," replied the head monk. "All you ever do is complain."

This story presents the paradox of a man who only voiced three complaints in 30 years yet never had a good word to say about anything.

I'd like you to try an experiment. See if you can go for a full day without complaining about anything. This means neither complaining to yourself (via your own thoughts) or others. This is not as easy as it may sound. If you catch yourself complaining, start over the next day. My guess is that it will take you quite awhile to have a full day and night of not having even one complaint.

But here's the good news. I'll bet you feel pretty good about it. And, I'll bet that some of your co-workers, friends, or family members feel good about it also. I don't mean to suggest that it's not all right to become frustrated or vent your feelings, but many of us are in the habit of complaining if things don't go smoothly or according to our plans. Take a day of being less judgmental, less reactive, less perfectionist, less smug, and less frustrated. Take a vacation from complaining. Hey, I'm really not asking that much of you! That monk could only complain once every ten years!

How To Deal With Your Demons

Remember the movie or book, <u>The Exorcist</u>. I would like to take it less literally and more metaphorically. By the time we are adults, we all possess personal "demons" that reside within us. These so called demons are born from a collection of negative experiences accumulated as we journey through life. They result from everything that we've thought or done that we may have felt ashamed of or embarrassed about, including all of our sins, crimes, and horrible fears. Transgressions, fantasies, or behaviors that have been labeled as bad by others or ourselves comprise our collections of personal demons. Intense feelings of guilt, hostility, and unacceptable sexuality reside in the daimonic.

Here's what I'd like you to know. Everyone's closet has demons. Don't believe that your secrets and your demons are unmatched by anyone else's. In that respect, as in many other respects, we are all more alike than different.

Most people fear their demons and try to deny or repress them or project them onto others. Paradoxically, the way to exorcise the demons is to accept them.

In the Tibetan Buddhist literature, you are told to embrace your 10,000 horrible demons. That translates to accepting that you are a fallible human being probably raised in something resembling a dysfunctional family in the midst of an often-confusing world where you've received conflicting messages and critical evaluation. You think that you're not enough

163

or that you're unworthy. You feel shame, guilt, hostility, self-ishness, and embarrassment. You may feel like an imposter. You may feel deviant. Understandable. Most of us have struggled with those thoughts and feelings.

I use the label "just stuff" whenever those thoughts or feelings try to haunt, taunt, frighten, or bully me. I won't indulge them or cling to them. I won't cower. I'll embrace my 10,000 demons. "Just stuff." I'll let go and move on. Try it.

The Meaning Of Life: Part II

I don't have it all figured out. I must admit, sometimes I don't have a clue. It's been said that the unexamined life is not worth living. It's not that I haven't examined life, but being certain there are correct answers to those examination questions is another story.

After struggling for answers to important metaphysical questions such as the nature of God and the meaning of life, I have reached one conclusion. That is, I don't want to obsess over those questions. At age 59, I don't know if there's a master plan, predetermination, or cosmic indifference. Edward R. Murrow once said (although I'm probably quoting him out of context) that "anyone who isn't confused really doesn't understand the situation".

What it gets down to for me is how I live my life each day and how I feel about my life. It gets down to how I love, how I treat people, and how I treat myself. R.H. Blyth once wrote, "We all know what is what, what to do, what not to do, but pretend we don't by means of asking questions about the meaning of life, the existence of God, and the immortality of the soul."

When the Indian government was about to expel Ram Dass from their country (visa problems), he knew time was of the essence. He had been sitting for years at the feet of his guru looking for The Answer. He begged the guru, who relented and handed him a mango. Ram Dass excitedly said to himself, "This is *the* mango!" He wasn't certain what to do with it. He didn't know if he should plant the seed or if the one piece would be enough. He hid it so he wouldn't have to share it. Finally, he ate the mango. Nothing happened. It was just a good mango.

Give Yourself a Break

A lecturer was invited to speak at a prison to an audience of hardened convicts. As she nervously approached the podium, she tripped and took a nasty fall. The convicts laughed unmercifully. Brushing the dirt from her suit, the speaker reached the microphone and stated, "The first point I'd like to make is that a person can fall flat on his face, get up, and start over." This message was particularly poignant to the group she was addressing.

We all make mistakes. I'm still amazed that maturity encompasses such a lengthy process. I imagine I'll feel even more mature at 60 than I do now. But being mature doesn't equal not making any mistakes. I don't berate myself if a decision I make doesn't always work out well. Sometimes we have to make decisions based on insufficient information. Sometimes we proceed by the seat of our pants. It is easy to be the proverbial Monday morning quarterback and see exactly what we should have done.

If you make a mistake, learn whatever you can from it, so that maybe when you find yourself in a similar circumstance you'll be able to make a decision you feel better about. In any event, do not beat yourself up for having made a mistake. William Durant, the founder of General Motors, put it this way: "Forget past mistakes. Forget failures. Forget everything except what you're going to do now and do it."

Seven Times Down, Eight Times Up

Failure isn't falling down. It's not getting up. If you fall down 100 times, get up 101. If you've made mistakes, admit them, apologize if necessary, realize you have another chance, and take positive action. Don't get discouraged. Get moving. Get started.

Make a Difference

There's a fairly large segment of the population that I have not given their due. It's only in recent years that I've truly come to appreciate the importance of them. I'm talking about volunteers. We take them for granted, but they deserve better. They come in all shapes, sizes, and ages, and their common purpose is to help others. They do this knowing they will not receive any pay for their services. Think about this. They give freely of their time specifically to help you and they don't want anything in return. That's a description of a group I would feel proud to be a part of. How about you?

There's a guy who volunteers his help at a nursing home where my wife Nan works. His name is Vince and he's about fifty years old. He was a construction worker for thirty years but can no longer do that work because of an injury that has left him with a pronounced limp. I see Vince in action on an almost daily basis. The residents of the home love him. He talks to them all and takes many of them outside to sit each day.

If Vince did not do this, the majority of these people would not get fresh air or the special affection he affords them. He speaks very loudly so they can hear him and jokes around with most of them. He frequently introduces residents to each other and tries to spur interactions between them. Although he doesn't get a dime, in my estimation, he's worth a fortune. I try not to confuse net-worth with self-worth. I respect Vince and try to learn from him.

Think about the volunteers you've experienced. Did someone push your wheelchair when you were in the hospital? Did someone hold out a cup of water to you at the two-mile mark of a local 5-K run? Think about becoming a volunteer. Whether it's five days a week or an hour or two a few times a year, you can make a difference!

John Wesley (founder of the Methodist Church) said:
> Do all the good you can
> By all the means you can
> In all the ways you can
> In all the places you can
> To all the people you can
> As long as ever you can.

<u>Keep a Journal</u>

I haven't kept a journal in over twenty years, but I still find valuable writings when I look through my old ones. And people tell me frequently that writing their thoughts, feelings, and experiences in a notebook helps them in various ways. Start by buying a notebook and a pen that feel right to you. This will be your private arena where anything and everything is permissible. When you write, it's unnecessary to censor, edit, or delete. You needn't be concerned with form, spelling, grammar, or punctuation. It is not going to be graded.

Trust yourself. Anything you write is acceptable. Go with your feelings. Give yourself permission. This is for your own benefit, not for anyone else's entertainment. Express yourself fully. Relinquish yourself to the pen and paper. Stream of consciousness is okay. Let it happen.

If you want to include future plans and goals, do it. Being logical is fine. Dreaming is also fine. Record dreams that seem to be important. Write about past events that had a major impact on you. How about your earliest recollections of anything? Fill in the blanks of the following questions and then expound upon your answers:

If it weren't for my _____, I'd
_____.

If I were less afraid, I would _____.

I really resent _____.

The most important thing in the world for me is

_____.

If I were totally independent, I would

_____.

If I could change one thing about me, it would be

_____.

I'd feel better if I _____.

Before I die, I would like to:

a)_____.

b)_____.

c)_____.

d)_____.

e)_____.

When you write, how long you write, and what you write are up to you. Define your own relationship to your journal. It's all about you and what's important enough to you to write about. Do it with passion.

Sadhana

Sadhana is a term that refers to working on yourself along the spiritual path. I've adapted it to include the psychological as well. So Sadhana is working on yourself along spiritual/psychological dimensions to help you obtain peace of mind, purpose, and meaning.

Early on, it is a very selective thing. You do Sadhana once or twice a week in your therapist's office or in yoga or tai chi class. You also do Sadhana in church, temple, mosques, and monasteries. Sadhana is reserved for workshops, retreats, and occasional other selected times and places.

A very interesting phenomenon occurs as you venture farther down the spiritual path. Distinctions begin to evaporate and boundary lines become blurred. The places for Sadhana are less exclusive. The time for Sadhana is more inclusive. It gets to the point that wherever you are and whatever you're doing, it's an opportunity to work on yourself.

Recently, I was a passenger in a car driven by a 52 year-old friend of mine. She was trying to merge into traffic and a car driven by a young man wouldn't let her in. She spontaneously and angrily gave him an obscene gesture. He returned the favor. He was at the age where he could have been her son and she his mother. It was a Sunday morning and both cars ended up in the same church parking lot where they were going to get religion/spirituality. This is an example of selective Sadhana.

The two drivers of the cars didn't experience themselves as being in OUR traffic jam. They were two very distinct and separate individual egos having little relationship with each other and no shared responsibility for participating in THIS together. They were not practicing Sadhana on the highway, only in the church.

If I'm doing Sadhana and so are you, then everyone in the entire universe is working on US.

> I am I
> And You are You
> And it may seem
> That We are Two
> But when it all
> Is said and done
> We will know
> There's only ONE.

Buckle Up

A friend asked me why I always wear a seat belt. It doesn't matter if I'm driving for five hours or five minutes, I put it on consistently. I once read the results of a study that compared seat belt users to non-seat belt users along numerous dimensions. The seat belt wearers exercised more, had more vitamin C and beta-carotene in their diets, and ate more fruits and vegetables. Those who didn't use seat belts smoked more and took less vitamin pills.

I think the reason I wear a seat belt is that I value life and value myself. I want to live and be in good health. Clicking that belt on is not a compulsive ritual, it's a conscious choice. That click equals "I care deeply about me, my loved ones, health, and life." I want to see my kids grow up. If they have kids, I want to be able to play with my grandchildren. There are many places I look forward to exploring. In other words, I'm going to try to stay healthy and alive by making choices such as snapping on that seat belt. I'll exercise regularly, eat my fruits and vegetables, take my vitamin pills and even avoid second hand smoke.

Do you love yourself? I ask that because I think that's the answer to the question my friend posed to me. Although I'm not Narcissus, I love myself. I thought I'd feel embarrassed saying that, but I don't. I feel good about saying it. I hope you can say that you love yourself, and I hope your choices reflect that.

Seven Times Down, Eight Times Up

If we all do a better job of taking care of ourselves, we'll all be in a better position to take care of each other.

<u>Never Give Up</u>

Many things in life are hard to do. But you can do hard things. If you've read the above lines in previous stories, it's because you need to get that message again and again. Because something is very difficult does not mean that it is beyond you. Let me repeat this. You are capable of doing very difficult things. If you believe in yourself and persevere, you'll be amazed at what you are capable of.

When I began college, I decided to try out for the basketball team. Although I did not play for my high school team, I had confidence in myself as a player. Most of the players in college were on scholarships. There would only be a couple of roster spots for what were called "walk-ons" or non-scholarship players. I worked hard at all the practices and made the team.

Before the season began, I did well in scrimmage games and worked myself up to being the 2nd or 3rd substitute off the bench. Then, running backwards at full speed during a drill, I fell and got a concussion. The season started and I was not in uniform. I missed a couple of weeks and began practicing again. By mid-season I was a starter and playing well. I never thought that I couldn't do it.

In the running community, there is a father and son team known as the Hoyts. They've participated in many races over a long period of time including a number of major marathons. A marathon is a grueling race of slightly more than 26 miles.

177

Many things can go wrong as you run that distance. Many do. It is a very challenging event.

The younger Hoyt has cerebral palsy and I think he is now 40 years old. He sits in a specially devised apparatus that is something akin to a wheelchair, while his father runs behind it pushing. Mr. Hoyt pushes his son the entire 26 miles in about 3 hours, going up and down steep hills such as Boston's infamous "heartbreak hill". It is inspirational to watch them, to witness the determination, courage, and spirit manifested that resides somewhere deep within us all.

About a year ago, I heard the story of a 91 year-old grandmother who decided to walk from California to New York. She did this to raise awareness regarding the need for presidential campaign finance reform. Her plan was to walk ten miles each day. She got ill in the middle of her journey and needed to be hospitalized. She persisted and completed her walk over the course of fourteen months. When interviewed afterward, her advice to others was, "Never give up. Never give up. Never give up the ship!"

You are capable of doing extraordinary things. You can get through difficult times. Believe in yourself and never give up. Never.

Looking from a Different Vantage Point

A Bodhisattva is a person who has reached enlightenment and has decided to help you reach enlightenment without your realizing that is what's going on. Legend has it that Bodhisattvas can assume an infinite number of roles and disguises in order to help set you free from the psychological and/or spiritual obstacles that hold you back and prevent you from reaching your Buddha nature (waking fully to life). Bodhisattvas continually present you with opportunities to work on yourself.

For example, if you get angry easily and that anger frequently causes problems for you, Bodhisattvas will arise every now and again to provide you with chances so as to learn how to handle your feelings differently. In this light, the guy who cuts you off while you are driving your car, the insurance salesman who persistently calls during dinner, or the person who's rude to you may all be regarded as Bodhisattvas.

Before you become enraged as usual, do a little flip around in your mind and see the situation from a rather different and unique vantage point. See the person as a Bodhisattva who is providing you with a chance to learn to deal differently with this usually troublesome situation. Now, you can smile and say to yourself, "Thank you Bodhisattva for this valuable opportunity."

179

Nicolo, Ann, and Sam

Nicolo Paganini was a gifted 19th century violinist. He was performing in Italy before a packed house and the memorable concert was going wonderfully. Suddenly, toward the end of the concert, a string on his violin snapped and hung limply from his instrument. Paganini, although startled, continued to play, improvising beautifully.

Then to everyone's surprise, a second string broke, and shortly thereafter, a third. Paganini stood there with three strings dangling from his Stradivarius. But instead of leaving the stage, he stood his ground and calmly completed the difficult number on the one remaining string.

Ann Landers, who has given a considerable amount of advice in her lifetime, stated the most useful advice she could give is this: "Expect trouble as an inevitable part of life and when it comes, hold your head high, look it squarely in the eye, and say, 'I will be bigger than you. You cannot defeat me.'"

Early in life, most of us have the equivalent of a full set of strings on our violin, so to speak. My brother Sam was smart and loved to debate. Everyone thought he'd make a wonderful lawyer. Circumstances were such that he had little formal schooling. He joined the army to see the world and wound up as a disabled veteran (the first string snapped). He married and had the son he always wanted. His son died suddenly at age 14 (string number two). Many other extremely difficult events and situations became grist for the mill in Sam's life.

Shortly before his 70th birthday, he was diagnosed with stage four metastatic cancer (there went the third string).

Sam was given three to four months to live. About 15 months later, our mother died in April, 2001. When we told Sam, he was in the hospital with end stage cancer and was in a debilitated state. We doubted he'd be able to go to the funeral. Like Paganini, Sam improvised on his one remaining string. Somehow, he managed to arrive at the funeral parlor, but that wasn't enough for him. Using a walker and with a bedpan in hand, he slowly got himself in position to deliver a stirring eulogy to our mother. He died the following month.

If you have all four strings on your violin, you are extremely fortunate. Realize that. Regardless of however many strings you have, you can improvise and play whatever music you are capable of playing. Remember Paganini and please remember my brother Sam.

<u>Whack</u>

Winston Churchill once said, "If you have an important point to make, don't try to be subtle or clever. Use a pile driver. Hit the point once. Then come back and hit it again. Then hit it a third time, a tremendous whack!"

Here's the point:

This is it!

This is not a dress rehearsal!

Think healthier. Take action.

Take responsibility for your feelings.

You are your choices.

You don't have time for

Bad moods, rage, guilt,

Anxiety, depression, or whining.

Everyday is important.

Instead of negative thinking,

Take positive action -

NOW!

(WHACK!)

Read that point again!!

(WHACK #2!)

Read it again!!!

(TREMENDOUS WHACK!)

<u>Enlightenment?</u>

To reach enlightenment is a goal of many seekers traversing the spiritual path. To solve the koan. To reach satori. I've met a number of enlightened Zen Masters, teachers, and students. And certainly there are many people who seemingly have reached enlightenment via other routes than Zen. I must confess that when people attain that lofty status of enlightenment, I'm a bit skeptical.

There's the story of the old monk who meditated on a mountaintop for nine years and had his satori experience. When he finally left the mountain and entered the marketplace, someone stepped on his foot and the monk screamed obscenities at him.

I'm not sure what this striving for satori is all about. R.H. Blyth raised the question as to whether enlightenment makes a man or a woman a better person. I like that question. Some beings that have professed to be enlightened have proven themselves to be sexist, bigoted, selfish, greedy, and manipulative. Maybe, it's my unrealistic expectations of what it means to be an enlightened person. After all, it's just a word, but it does connote some kind of more-than-human qualities.

I guess the bottom line for me is that enlightenment isn't a guarantee of anything. I used to think it was. In fact, I once actively sought it by attending a three-day intensive meditation retreat where I did sitting meditation (zazen) at a Zen temple (zendo). I wrote the following haiku sequence about my experience. A haiku is a brief, non-metaphorical, non-embellished poem depicting the present moment.

removing shoes
before entering the zendo -
hole in my sock

zazen:
every now and then
silence breaks the noise

twelve hours now
not feeling the pain
in my legs

just breathing in
just breathing out –
this runny nose

breakfast
fourteen people
and no words

on the toilet
emptying my bowels
and my mind

today
even my fart
is silent

        spider
        on my zazen cushion –
        looking for enlightenment?

        the long day...
        even the Zen Master
        uses the toilet

        driving home
        feeling close to satori
        a car cuts me off

   I guess to me, enlightenment is something akin to bringing your consciousness and spirit fully to whatever you are
doing at the moment. Investing your self 100% in washing
those pots and pans instead of thinking that once this chore is
over with I can do something I want to do.
   Participating fully as best as you can with as much zest
as you can in a conscious and responsible manner. Not being
preoccupied with yourself, but becoming one with whatever
you're doing. Taizan Maezumi Roshi calls this "to forget the
self" and "to be enlightened by all things".

Jenna and Her Bag of Troubles

I want to remind you of the importance of choosing carefully to what you pay attention. Don't become preoccupied with pessimism or negativity. If it seems or feels as if the world is upside down, a paradigm shift in how you perceive the world would be helpful. Try the vantage point of thankfulness as you embrace each day. Landing on your feet is a choice you are capable of making. If it is 'seven times down', it is 'eight times up'.

There is a children's book about Jenna and her bag of troubles. Jenna is told to put all her troubles in a large bag and take this bag to a huge field where everyone else has brought their own bags of trouble. She is given the opportunity to look through all the bags that have been left there and to choose one to take back home with her. She spends all night sifting through all the bags and finally chooses one. As it turns out, Jenna chose her own bag of troubles, the bag she brought to the field in the first place.

Take five or ten minutes a day to pause and express your gratitude for everything that you have and for the fact that you've been given another day.

The Whole Ball of Wax

In an ideal world, life would be fair. But life is neither fair nor not fair, it simply is. Children die. Terrible things happen. There are terrorists, kidnappers, rapists, and murderers. There's also love, family, friendships, discovery, joy, and compassion. That's the way it is. We have to take the whole ball of wax. It's all inseparable.

Life and death, horrible and wonderful, big and little, ugly and beautiful, rich and poor, and black and white are all like stick 'em notes. We label as we judge events and objects. We divide the world into separate entities. But, in reality, there's only one stick 'em note labeled "the whole ball of wax". The world is exactly as it is.

I value happiness. I think that's what most of us want. A big part of achieving that is to understand the ancient Zen teaching that all we ever do in life is go from one Holy Place to another. It's all Creation. All God. It's all the Universe. It's all Nature. Everything is part of it and that's IT. The garbage too. Those are the labels we use when we divide the ball of wax. Of course we'll continue to strive for a fairer, better, less evil world. In the meantime, try for less and less categories, judgments, and stick 'em notes.

It's almost as if whatever happens, you say, "That's part of IT too." When you buy that brand new, shiny, seemingly indestructible SUV, understand and accept that it will inevitably become old, faded, and dented. Then, when it is first scraped in the supermarket parking lot, you'll say, "Yes, that's part of it too." You enjoy the SUV new even though it's already decomposing as you buy it (as does everything and everybody). And that's pretty much what life is like. We treasure it no matter what comes our way because it's all part of the whole ball of wax.

Works Cited

Becker, Ernest. <u>The Denial of Death</u>. New York: The Free Press, 1973.

Beckett, Samuel. <u>Waiting For Godot</u>. 1954. New York: Grove Press, 1997.

Bellissimo, A. and E. Tunks. <u>Behavioral Medicine: Concepts and Procedures</u>. New York: Pergamon, 1991.

Bittner, Herbert. <u>Kaethe Kollwitz Drawings</u>. Cranbury, NJ: Thomas Yoseloff Publisher, 1959.

Blyth, R.H. <u>Zen and Zen Classics: Volume One</u>. 1960. Tokyo: The Hukuseido Press, 1962.

Blyth, R.H. <u>Zen and Zen Classics: Volume Two</u>. Tokyo: The Hukuseido Press, 1964.

Blyth, R.H. <u>Zen and Zen Classics: Volume Three</u>. Tokyo: The Hukuseido Press, 1970.

Blyth, R.H. <u>Zen and Zen Classics: Volume Four</u>. 1966. Tokyo: The Hukuseido Press, 1978.

Blyth, R.H. <u>Zen and Zen Classics: Volume Five</u>. 1962. Tokyo: The Hukuseido Press, 1966.

Camus, Albert. <u>The Myth of Sisyphus and Other Essays</u>. 1955. New York: Vintage Books, 1991.

Carroll, Lewis. <u>Alice In Wonderland</u>. 1951. New York: Washington Square Press, 1976.

Castaneda, Carlos. <u>Journey To Ixtlan</u>. 1972. New York: Washington Square Press, 1992.

Cutler, H.C. and Dalai Lama. <u>The Art of Happiness: A Handbook For Living</u>. New York: Riverhead Books, 1998.

Dass, Ram. <u>Grist For the Mill</u>. 1976. Berkeley: Celestial Arts, 1988.

Dass, Ram. <u>The Only Dance There Is</u>. 1974. Northvale, NJ: Jason Aronson, 1979.

De Martino, R., Fromm, E., and D.T. Suzuki. <u>Zen Buddhism and Psychoanalysis</u>. New York: Harper and Row, 1970.

English, J. and G. Feng. <u>Lao Tsu: Tao Te Ching</u>. New York: Vintage Books, 1972.

Fields, R. and B. Glassman. <u>Instructions to the Cook: A Zen Master's Lessons In Living a Life That Matters</u>. New York: Bell Tower, 1996.

Frankl, Victor. <u>Man's Search For Meaning</u>. 1946. New York: Washington Square Press, 1997.

Gettis, Alan. <u>Sun Faced Haiku Moon Faced Haiku</u>. Battle Ground, IN: High/Coo Press, 1982.

Guntrip, Harry. Schizoid Phenomena, Object Relations, and the Self. 1969. Madison, CT: International Universities Press, 2001.

Hanh, Thich Nhat. Teachings On Love. Berkeley, CA: Parallax Press, 1998.

Johnson, Richard E. Existential Man: The Challenge of Psychotherapy. New York: Pergamon, 1971.

Jourard, Sidney. The Transparent Self. New York: D. Van Nostrand Co., 1971.

Kierkegaard, Soren. Concluding Unscientific Postscript. 1941. Princeton, NJ: Princeton University Press, 1992.

Kopp, Sheldon. If You Meet the Buddha On the Road…Kill Him! 1972. New York: Bantam, 1988.

Laing, R.D. The Politics of Experience. New York: Pantheon, 1967.

Luciani, Joseph J. Self-Coaching: How To Heal Anxiety and Depression. New York: John Wiley & Sons, Inc., 2001.

Maezumi, Hakuyu Taizan. The Way of Everyday Life. Los Angeles: Center Publications, 1978.

Maslow, Abraham. The Farther Reaches of Human Nature. 1971. Esalen Books, 1993.

May, Rollo. Freedom and Destiny. 1981. New York: W.W. Norton, 1999.

May, Rollo. <u>Love and Will</u>. New York: W.W. Norton & Co., 1969.

Menahem, Sam. <u>When Therapy Isn't Enough: The Healing Powers of Prayer and Psychotherapy</u>. Winfield, IL: Relaxed Books, 1995.

Menahem, Sam. <u>All Your Prayers Are Answered</u>. Lincoln, NE: Writer's Digest, 2000.

Mitchell, Stephen. <u>Dropping Ashes On the Buddha</u>. 1976. New York: Grove Press, 1994.

Nall, Sam. <u>It's Only a Mountain: Dick and Rick Hoyt – Men of Iron</u>. St. Petersburg, FL: Southern Heritage Press, 2002.

Perls, Fritz. <u>In and Out of the Garbage Pail</u>. Lafayette, CA: Real People Press, 1969.

Reps, Paul. <u>Zen Flesh, Zen Bones: A Collection of Zen and Pre-Zen Writings</u>. Boston: Shambhala, 1994.

Suzuki, Shunryu. <u>Zen Mind, Beginner's Mind</u>. New York: John Weatherhill, Inc., 1973.

Salinger, J.D. <u>Raise High the Roof Beam Carpenters and Seymour, An Introduction</u>. 1963. New York: Back Bay Books, 2001.

Trungpa, Chugyam. <u>Cutting Through Spiritual Materialism</u>. 1973. Boston: Shambhala, 2002.

Watts, Alan. <u>Out of the Trap</u>. South Bend, IN: And Books, 1985.

Watts, Alan. <u>The Way of Zen</u>. 1957. New York: Vintage Books, 1999.

ISBN 1412005140

9 781412 005142